ETERNITY

Eternity

Where will you spend it?

Russ Walsh

Xulon Press

Xulon Press
2301 Lucien Way #415
Maitland, FL 32751
407.339.4217
www.xulonpress.com

© 2018 by Russ Walsh

All rights reserved solely by the author. The author guarantees all contents are original and do not infringe upon the legal rights of any other person or work. No part of this book may be reproduced in any form without the permission of the author. The views expressed in this book are not necessarily those of the publisher.

Scripture quotations taken from the Holy Bible, New International Version (NIV). Copyright © 1973, 1978, 1984, 2011 by Biblica, Inc.™. Used by permission. All rights reserved.

Printed in the United States of America.

ISBN-13: 9781545636190

Table of Contents

Preface. ix
Introduction xvii
Chapter 1: Is There a Creator/God?. 1
Chapter 2: Who Is This Creator/God? 36
Chapter 3: Why Were We Created?. 52
Chapter 4: Why Is the World Full of
           Problems? 68
Chapter 5: The Bible: Adam to the
           Tower of Babel 96
Chapter 6: The Bible: Who Was Abraham?. . . 105
Chapter 7: The Bible: Abraham to Moses 116
Chapter 8: States of the Heart 128
Chapter 9: The Bible: The Nation of Israel . . . 148
Chapter 10: Who is Jesus? 158
Chapter 11: What Happens After We Die? . . . 179
Chapter 12: Who Can Be Saved? 193

Chapter 13: Time to Make a Change? 205
Chapter 14: A New Life 217
Suggested Sources. 239
About the Author. 251

Preface

Moments That Transform Us

We live in a world where technology continually affects how we live our lives. It was 1995, and I had just gotten my first laptop computer. I started using a word-processing software product from a fairly young company called Microsoft, and I was fascinated by the power I had to easily create documents that looked like they were produced at a printing press. Prior to that, creating a document with various font sizes and colors actually required building a software program around the document's content--on a computer that cost about $100,000. Suddenly, I found myself using my own personal computer that cost about $1000, and I was able to do many new things, including writing a book. This was a moment in time that transformed me.

Technology has come a long way since 1995. Recently, glasses were invented that allow a color-blind person to see in color. I first discovered that this technology exists in 2016 by watching a post on Facebook. A family made a video clip via their Apple iPhone of their 60-year old dad (and granddad) getting these special glasses on his birthday and seeing in color for the first time in his life. At the start of the video, this tough rugged-looking man was smiling and having fun, but he was unsure of this interesting gift. When he put on those glasses, he immediately removed them and tears welled up in his eyes. He totally lost his composure. After a minute or so—and several rounds of wiping his eyes—he put on the glasses again, but he still couldn't keep them on but a few seconds. He began weeping harder as he tried to comprehend that a long-held dream of seeing the world in color had actually come true in his lifetime. This was a moment that transformed him.

Preface

They say that most of us only retain a small amount of information from the books that we read. I can attest to that. I've read many books, including classics, such as C.S. Lewis' *Mere Christianity*, in writing this book. However, a few days or weeks after reading most books, I can only remember a few high-level concepts and some of the stories or analogies that were presented.

It is also said that most of us don't remember everything that we're told, but that we never forget how people made us feel. With that in mind, most readers won't retain every fact and story that I'm about to share. Nevertheless, I hope this book makes you feel that it was written to you by someone who cares deeply about you.

We live in a world with lots of confusion over what is true and what is not and whether there is any real truth at all. As a result, we often find ourselves going through life with little regard about the truly important matters, such as why we exist and what happens to us after we die. This book has the answers to some of life's toughest issues and is a culmination of more than two decades of research and more than five decades of observing life on this planet. It references many of the most powerful books ever written, including scientific and spiritual research by many renowned experts.

I have an engineering degree and have spent the past two decades working in the world's technology hub, the Silicon Valley region of California's San Francisco Bay Area. I have worked with nearly every major technology firm of our day, including Apple, Google, Oracle, IBM, Facebook, Amazon, GE, Uber, Hitachi, and Microsoft. I have had the privilege of working with some of the world's most well-educated leaders, many of them graduates of Ivy League universities such as Harvard, Princeton, and MIT. I have discussed many of life's most important issues with some of these brilliant people, and this book addresses many difficult questions and insights they have posed. Interestingly, many of their questions and insights aren't much different from typical people whom I've met during my life. Often, I find that the more educated that people become, the less they sometimes understand very basic truths.

PREFACE

While many books have been written over the centuries about topics that address spirituality and God, science and our world's origins, good and evil, and love and hate, I hope this book will weave all of these important components in a way that will give new insights into the most critical matters of life, death, and eternity. I hope you will read this with an open mind and an open heart. Just as the story of the man who saw color for the first time, I hope this book touches you in a very special way such that your life and eternal destination are forever impacted. Even if you already agree with the general perspective of what I'm about to present, perhaps this book will be something you can share with others you care about that will deeply transform their life and their destiny as well.

I once read a passage from a certain book, and 20 minutes later, my life was never the same. This book, **Eternity - Where will you spend it?** may not have that direct effect on you, but it will reference the Bible, which is the book that truly opened up my eyes and allowed me to see and finally understand the truth about this life and what awaits us all after our life on this earth ends. I hope this book will lead you to the Bible—the book that truly is the most special book ever written and truly changes hearts and minds.

Note

If you're finding yourself intrigued about the Old Testament topics that I won't be covering in this book, you can read about them in the Bible. If you need help getting a study Bible, refer to the Suggested Resources at the end of this book. If you need help finding a church in your area, please email me at russ@sc-love.org, and I will try to follow up with you within a few days.

Acknowledgments

I am very grateful to the people who took time to review this book and assist me in finding much of the information that I used as my sources. Several well-respected religious leaders from various Christian denominations directly or indirectly provided me with substantial portions of the information used in this book. One of the leading attorneys in America, Brad Dacus, President of the Pacific Justice Institute, reviewed this book and has endorsed it. Also, several Christian pastors, Christian book editors, and other respected religious leaders reviewed drafts of this book and responded that the viewpoints I present are valid and agree with fundamental Christian doctrine. Also, material from many Christian publications and radio programs were used, such as Dr. Billy Graham's ministry, Dr. J. Vernon McGee's "Through the Bible" ministry, Dr. Charles Swindoll's "Insight for Living" ministry, "Focus on the Family" Christian ministry broadcasts, and Dr. Ravi Zacharias' "Ravi Zacharias International Ministry" also known as RZIM.

In addition, this book has been reviewed by several other Christians and non-Christians, professional editors and a Christian book publisher and their feedback and insights were also extremely helpful.

I want it to be clear, however, that the viewpoints I will be sharing in some areas are simply my opinion, and I welcome you to analyze my ideas and perspectives carefully. I also wrote this book using terminology that even children can understand because I believe that young children are completely capable of grasping much more about good and evil and life and death issues than we often want to give them credit for. My original draft of this book in 1997 was written primarily for my two daughters—aged two and six at that time. I wanted to ensure that I had documented and conveyed this important information about life, death, and eternity to these two very important little ones whom God had blessed me with the privilege of raising.

In summary, this book explains in straightforward terms what awaits us when our life on this earth ends and how we can secure our eternal destiny and impact the eternal destiny of others. I strongly recommend that the interested reader explore the sources that are listed at the back of this book to gain a deeper insight and belief regarding these crucial matters.

Introduction

What's the best news you could imagine hearing? You won the lottery! The person of your dreams wants to marry you! Your child overcame a deadly illness! You found the fountain of youth!

What's the worst news that you could imagine hearing? The plane you're flying on is about to crash! Your spouse is having an affair! Your child just died!

What if you could live forever in paradise, surrounded by the most loving, caring people you have shared your life with, along with your ancestors and their most loving and caring friends and family members? What if you died and found that there really is a place called hell where evil people were banished to forever?

What if you could find the meaning of life? What if you discovered your purpose for being here on earth? What if you learned where you will spend eternity—if there is such a thing? As stated earlier, I hope **Eternity - Where Will You Spend It?** will help you find the answers to life's toughest issues and most important questions.

There are many things that can concern people during the day to day experiences of life, but there is one issue that truly deserves ultimate consideration. Since no one who was alive on this planet two hundred years ago is still physically alive on earth today, it is very unlikely that any of us will be physically alive hundreds of years from now. Therefore, it seems that it would be useful to explore what might happen to each of us after our life on this planet ends. There are a number of ideas that have been proposed about life after death—such as ongoing reincarnation into new persons or even animals, a tranquil but somewhat boring place of clouds and angels, a terrifying place of fire and devils, or simply non-existence. This book addresses the matter of what awaits us after our physical life ends and what determines our eternal destination. Although it is not popular in this day and time to say that someone's beliefs are wrong, these vastly different perspectives of the future indicate that all of these beliefs cannot be correct. This book is based on trustworthy sources that go far beyond just hopeful fantasies that someone may have dreamed up and passed onto others.

While some people claim to have experienced some glimpse into life after death, there really is no scientifically verifiable way at this point in history to bring closure to this matter. No one has found a way to peel back the curtain or open the door to the other side—if such a place even exists—and hold the curtain or door open long enough for everyone to have a chance to analyze this place for themselves. Therefore, the fundamental premise of this book is not something that can be proven or rejected in a laboratory, but rather, it requires an evaluation based on extensive examination, personal experience, and other factors that I will explain as we go through the book.

Basically then, my premise—as well as any other premise about this subject—is somewhat like a puzzle with a few pieces missing. I do not, however, believe that the missing pieces are significant enough to undermine the basic answers that I propose, otherwise I would not have bothered to develop this book. For example, if you looked out the front window of a small house and noticed that the ground was heavily covered with freshly fallen snow, it would be fairly safe to assume that you would see snow in other parts of your yard if you looked out other windows of your house.

As another example, how much evidence would you need to believe that London, England, exists? Do you have to experience London for yourself or are there other sources that are trustworthy, such as friends who have been there, books that refer to it, and airlines that sell tickets for people who plan to travel there? Similarly, I am illustrating a glimpse into eternity for you that is taken from trustworthy sources and clearly shows a significant portion of

INTRODUCTION

the final picture of the afterlife. Ultimately, I leave it up to you to draw your own conclusions.

My fundamental belief is that the Bible of the Christian religion is correct in its explanation of who God is, mankind's history on this earth, and the future that awaits us. There is a vast array of issues that need to be addressed for most people to come to this conclusion, such as the overall trustworthiness of a book written and translated over thousands of years, the belief that science has determined that our world came together without any intervention from a creative being, and the fate of people uninformed about the Christian religion. At this point in time, very few books are available that deeply address each of these critical concerns, so I felt it would be beneficial to consolidate some of the excellent research materials and insights that I have found into one comprehensive presentation.

While I am not going to attempt to address every question that you may be able to conceive regarding spirituality, science, and religion, I will try to supply enough information about issues pertaining to the matter of life after death to substantiate my premise.

For instance, I will not debate whether there is life on other planets, because the information we have today is both inconclusive and provides limited value to the discussion of life after death. I will, however, include details on certain relevant subjects—some of which have had little written about them to date. I will provide current scientific information that strongly indicates that most aspects of our world must have been created and could not have evolved in a natural, progressive fashion. I will also address the matter of whether only Christians will spend eternity in heaven.

The issue of whether any religion is false can be very sensitive, especially to someone who is a member of such a religion. Fortunately, however, my conclusions as taken from the bible do not indicate that people will be condemned for belonging to a certain religious group, but rather that each person will be judged as an individual. Nevertheless, false religions are very dangerous because they often confuse their followers' views about spiritual matters to the point that these people never realize their need to to be reconciled with God. I hope you will find that this book sheds valuable insight on an important subject that has been neglected for too long.

This book is based heavily upon my belief that the original Hebrew and Greek manuscripts that make up the Bible are free from error and represent the consolidation of writings inspired by the God and creator of this world. I am not fluent in Greek or Hebrew, and it is likely that you, the reader, are not fluent in either language either. We are fortunate, however, to have reliable translations of the Bible written in the same language that this book is written—English. Many Christian scholars believe—as I do—that the King James, the New International Version (NIV), and the New American Standard (NASB) versions of the Bible are trustworthy, inerrant translations of older versions of the Bible and can be taken literally. Since the King James Version was written centuries ago, its text can be more difficult to read than the more modern NIV and NASB versions. I really like both the NIV and NASB versions, but I, and many other Christian scholars whom I respect, generally prefer the NIV. Therefore, whenever this book makes a reference to the Bible, it will use quotations from the NIV version. As we go through the book, I will provide substantial evidence to support my belief as to why the Bible is trustworthy. Also, because I believe the Bible is truly inspired by God, the creator of this world, I will refer to God and the Bible with the first letter capitalized to emphasize respect and honor to both.

While this book includes detailed information and insights not found in the Bible, this supplementary information should not be assumed to contradict basic biblical principles. Although the Bible is complete in providing the information we need to understand basic spiritual matters, it does not seem that God intended it as the only book that should ever be written or read. In fact, the Bible has much less information about certain subjects than many people realize.

For instance, the Christian religion—as well as many other religions—place a great deal of emphasis on devils and demons. While I believe that these beings do exist and significantly influence our world, they are rarely mentioned in explicit detail except

Introduction

in Revelation, the final book of the Bible and in the third chapter of the first book of the Bible, Genesis. The first half of the Bible, called the Old Testament, has only a few references to demons and the devil. The Bible refers to the devil as Satan, Lucifer, and many other names. Throughout this book, I will refer to him as the devil unless there is reason to indicate differently.

While most of the second half of the Bible, called the New Testament, has only limited references to the devil and these demons, the stories it does contain strongly indicate that people knew much about them. In fact, the New Testament describes how Jesus encountered several people who were actually possessed by demons. The point is that sometimes the Bible does not explain certain important things in long detail. The Bible often leaves it up to us to develop explanations based on what information it provides—along with our own insights and experiences—and some of these interpretations may be documented for others to refer to in the future. In this case, the people of Jesus' time knew a lot more about demonic beings than the Old Testament of the Bible had told them. They had other sources, teachings, and experiences to add to their basic biblical knowledge.

As we go through this book, the issue of what awaits us after our physical life is over will be dealt with in a progressive manner, wherein I will first build some basis for believing that a god or gods might actually exist before I progress to the next section where we will discuss the Bible and determine whether it truly was inspired by some god. I will explain mankind's origins and the events that led to the formation of a special nation called Israel. I will also explain how Israel's role in the writing of the Old Testament significantly enhances the reliability that the Bible is truly God's message to mankind. Dozens of religious and political figures in Israel contributed to this amazing God-inspired collection of writings that carefully document the historical and supernatural events that our ancestors witnessed.

The Old Testament also contains detailed predictions of future events, many of which have been accurately fulfilled. Writings from the Bible written

INTRODUCTION

thousands of years ago mention that someday men would fly through the air in thundering 'locusts with the faces of men,' which sounds a lot like a helicopter. More importantly, the Bible predicted more than 3,000 years ago that someday God himself would actually come to live, die, and then rise from the dead in the person of Jesus Christ. It also predicts that Jesus Christ will come again someday, but instead of a humble baby born in stable, his next appearance will give him the role of king of the entire earth.

We then will analyze the Bible to determine why God created us and how the special free will that He has given to angels and human beings has led to our world becoming both a wonderful place and a difficult place to enjoy living in. We will also examine what the Bible says about why our physical life is limited and whether there is life after death. Most importantly, we will discuss how our basic attitude and relationship with God affects our eternal destiny.

We will next take a quick peek into the Bible's illustrations of the afterlife as it is presently and of the afterlife in its final state after the world—as we currently know it—comes to an end.

My background does not include a formal degree from a religious institution. However, it does include an electrical/computer engineering degree, working for more than three decades as a computer information systems practitioner, being the CEO of software and consulting companies in Silicon Valley, being a husband and father for more than two decades, having a lifetime of involvement with Christian religious denominations, and researching the topics that this book addresses for countless hours.

I have found that many adults—and even quite a few young people—have put forth a significant amount of their own time and energy contemplating or researching these matters as well, but have encountered stumbling blocks that have frustrated their efforts to the point that only doubts and confusion remained. Since I also have experienced stumbling blocks at times, I thought that it would be beneficial to share insights and information that helped break through my confusion and doubt.

Introduction

In the late 1800s and early 1900s, many people were applying the latest technology and science to develop the ability to fly. Most of their ideas failed. However, on December 17, 1903, the world's ability to transport people and goods forever changed when the Wright brothers made four successful flights in North Carolina. Likewise, my hope is that this book will be a mechanism that transforms how people understand God and ultimately will transport many people into an eternal friendship with God.

Before I undertook the challenge of putting my own book together, I had hoped that I would simply find one or two books that sufficiently addressed the key issues so that I could refer these books to my friends, family, and church. Instead, I found that putting my own book together was the only way that I could answer questions and tough issues brought up by my friends, family members, and others I have encountered. It was also the most effective way to document and convey my understanding and findings to people whom I care greatly about, including my children—and hopefully someday grandchildren and descendants after them. Although it is nearly

ETERNITY

impossible to discuss life, death, and moral issues without evoking great emotion, this book will try to avoid confrontational situations as much as possible. It will also put more emphasis on presenting insightful analogies to address these issues rather than using formal theology. I have found that such formal rhetoric often does not clearly or quickly answer the important questions we may have. I also will present this material in a more personal style, using pronouns such as I, you, we, and us because I believe the personal method is the most effective way to discuss issues of this nature.

While I do not expect anyone to completely agree with every perspective I will share regarding these matters, I do hope that you will find useful information in the following pages. This book is intended to provide you with or strengthen your hope that this life can bring you great joy now and throughout eternity. You can have a personal friendship with the God and creator of this world who loves you, your family, your friends, and even your enemies more than we as human beings can possibly imagine. In addition, I hope that this book also energizes believers to share this message with those they care about because the Bible indicates that eternal agony and suffering await anyone who fails to accept God's love and friendship. While there are other factors that affect the eternal destiny of people, such as the age of accountability and the need to ask God for forgiveness, I will address the intricacies of these factors as this book progresses. Finally, I hope that this book causes those who are still skeptical to further invest time and energy to resolving their questions and issues.

Note

I will refer to the Bible throughout this book. If you are not familiar with the Bible, it is made up of sections called books, where each book generally is organized as sequentially numbered chapters and each chapter then has sequential numbering for almost every paragraph or sentence. The Christian Bible is broken up into sixty-six books with Genesis being the first book and Revelation being the last book. The Bible includes what is referred to as the

Old Testament, which contains the first thirty-nine books. The Old Testament was written between about 1500 BC and 400 BC. The Christian Bible also includes what's referred to as the New Testament, which contains the remaining twenty-seven books. The New Testament was written between about 45 AD and 90 AD. The Jewish people—the people of the nation of Israel—were the authors of the Old Testament, but the Jewish people who did not become Christians have generally never accepted the New Testament as being from God, and their Bible therefore just contains the Old Testament books.

Chapter 1

Is There a Creator/God?

*L*ife can be funny at times. I have a friend who always seems to have unusual things happen to her that are hard to explain, but they often seem to indicate that somewhere out there exists some behind-the-scenes being who has a sense of humor. For instance, she once needed to direct someone to meet her at an office building. She looked out the window of that building, noticed that the sign out front was badly damaged and had been for a long time. "It's the building with the sign that looks like a car smashed it, you can't miss it." she told the person. A few minutes later, she glanced out the building and saw three men loading the damaged sign onto a truck. Since this was before the days of cell phones, her meeting got started a little late that day.

But is there truly a behind-the-scenes being or god out there? We live in a world with many different points of view on this matter. In the 1990s, Andy Rooney from the CBS *60 Minutes* show said on one particular episode, "You would have to be foolish to believe in God. " He next stated, "You would have to be foolish not to believe in God." He, like many, could not agree with himself on the matter, so it is no wonder we cannot agree with others either. Mr. Rooney's statement is partially correct, for we all behave somewhat foolishly at times. However, he does not state whether or not he believes in God. His response was appropriate for our politically correct society. Today, we rarely ask meaningful questions and fail to recognize useless answers rather than asking thought-provoking questions wherein correct answers can be of great value.

You can ignore the issue of whether there really is a God if you want. Nevertheless, this is probably mankind's most fundamental issue. If there is no God, then there is basically no spiritual aspect to life. If there is no God and no spiritual aspect to life, then there is no life after death and there is no judgment after death to worry about—although it is funny that our ability to worry is actually a spiritual matter. If there is no creative being(s) who may somehow hold us accountable for our lives, then we can live our lives for purely selfish pleasures with concern for others only when it keeps us from being harmed or if it will be beneficial to us at some later time in our physical life on this planet. If, however, there is a God and a spiritual aspect to life, we are faced with at least four eternal outcomes that await us after death: heaven, hell, nothing, or something else.

Science, however, has resolved the matter of God and spirituality, or at least that is what many want to believe or claim to believe. According to some, the world all came together by chance and evolutionary processes. Now before I venture into the debate of whether science proves or disproves the existence of God, I want to make it clear that I think science cannot decide this matter. Nevertheless, I do want to take a look at the current facts that science presents regarding this matter. It seems that the general public has been given confusing information, causing many to believe that science and religion are competing philosophies. Part of the reason for the controversy is that the first part of the Bible—the Book of Genesis, Chapters 1 and 2—seems to indicate that the world was created in just a six-day period within the past 6,000 to 10,000 years. Since many scientists do believe that the radioactive decay technologies used to estimate the age of fossils and geological formations indicate that the world is potentially somewhat or even much older than that, it may seem that science does threaten the credibility of the Bible. This point of conflict causes some people to believe that all discussions of the Bible and spirituality are unreliable. Therefore, I will venture briefly into this science and religious debate with hopes of at least imparting a better understanding of the issues and facts. I want to point out again that the objective of this discussion will not be—in and of itself—to prove or disprove the existence of God but rather to inject information into the discussion that may eliminate some of the confusion regarding the science and religion debate.

Before I venture into the specifics of evolution and creation, let us quickly analyze a couple of key points about the six-day creation story. The book of Genesis states that the sun, moon, and stars were not created until the fourth day of creation. Since the earth was somewhat alone prior to day four, it seems that the 24-hour system for measuring a day was somewhat meaningless because that system is based on the earth rotating relative to its surroundings. In addition, there were apparently no galactic surroundings until day four, so the time measuring system as we now know it could not have been relevant. Therefore, these first days actually could have been just a few minutes, or millions, or even billions of years.

On the other hand, the Bible also states that the first man, Adam, and all of the land animals were created on the sixth day. Other passages of the Bible —for example, Matthew 1:1–17 and Luke 3:23–38— trace all generations from Adam, the first created person, to Jesus in a timeline that most historians believe covers only about four to eight thousand years. This timeline also seems to cover about sixty to eighty total generations. If it is also true that Jesus lived about two thousand years ago, then we can conclude that it has only been about six to ten thousand years since day six of the creation story.

Now, let us analyze a couple of points regarding what science tells us about how old the earth is and how long mankind has existed. It is important to keep in mind an important understanding of what science is when we analyze the origins of mankind. It is not the job of science to take theories that are highly speculative and present them as absolute facts or fundamental truths—although this happens quite often in American society today. Rather, science is a tool that helps us gauge what might happen based on information we have gathered about things that have occurred or things that continue to occur.

For instance, if animal fossils are found buried in volcanic ash in a location above the ruins of a city that was documented as being covered by volcanic ash three hundred years ago, then it may be safe to conclude that the animal species was buried under the ash three hundred years ago or sometime within the past three hundred years. Also, modern science can accurately tell us the course that certain comets have followed over the past several decades and they can carry that accuracy back hundreds of years if they can match their projections to documented position data that was recorded by reliable scientific establishments centuries earlier. While scientists of our day can accurately speculate on future trajectories of these comets, it is not the job of scientists to dogmatically make statements in documentaries such as "fish grew legs and became land-dwelling animals 33,208,000 years ago." With current technology and the documentation provided by civilizations of the past, science is far short of presenting a reasonable case to support this event occurring at all—let alone having an exact date to tie it to.

Current scientific technology and mathematical principles used in estimating the age of geological and biological matter have the potential to be very accurate for dates within the past four thousand years. Since there are civilizations on this planet that we know existed during that time frame, we can take specimens that we can associate to specific dates in the past to verify those age-estimation principles. When we go beyond that time period, however, we lose the ability to correlate age theories with documented events, so the accuracy becomes more speculative over longer ranges of projections.

At this point, the mystery begins. On the one hand, science claims to have found geological formations calculated to be ten thousand times older than other similar geological formations known to be only three thousand years old. This would indicate that the material was somewhere between three thousand years old and thirty million years old, a large discrepancy for those who believe our earth is less than ten thousand years old. In addition, it is difficult to argue for a young earth when we can see light from stars that are millions of light years from earth. On the other hand, while modern society has made incredible strides over the past decades and centuries towards understanding many mysteries of how our world works, there has been little progress at all in understanding how or why things came into existence.

Since American academic culture today generally correlates a scientific perspective of our world's origins to be based on evolutionary principles, I will try to bring this science verses creation discussion towards to a point of closure by addressing a widely accepted evolution theory and the Bible's account of creation separately.

Note

I have had some readers tell me that the following section is unnecessary because they can't understand how anyone could question the existence of God. For anyone who is not interested in the details of this discussion, please feel free at any time to move around through this book to sections that interest you most. Likewise, even if you are convinced that this topic does not have relevance to you, it may be helpful for you to understand this section in case you someday encounter conversations with people, including family members or friends, who don't believe in God because of what they've been taught or haven't been taught about this issue.

Natural Evolution

While science has yet to present any reasonable hypothesis about where matter originally came from, many scientists today believe this general concept.

> A big bang occurred about 13 billion years ago that eventually led to an evolutionary formation of stars, planets, etc. Then, energy forces led to biological formations on this planet which could be mutated, altered, and adapted over time into other more complex biological forms.

Whether our world came to be in this way or not, no one can be sure. Geological formations and fossilized remains of plants and animals in some ways seem to support the idea of an evolutionary development of our planet, but these same fossil findings also cast doubt on this idea because the findings to date do not show the expected gradual differences between similar species from supposedly different eras. Instead, it shows completely developed life forms with rather substantial differences from other similar life forms, indicating great skips in development that cannot easily be explained. Just think about certain winged creatures such as the ostrich, the peacock, and the butterfly. You would expect there to be dozens or even thousands of similar creatures between these species and other typical winged species such as the robin or the crow. However, these three species are amazingly unique. The fossil records do not explain their uniqueness or any transitional process to derive them from any intermediate species.

More importantly, science cannot come close to providing specific details of how even the most basic of biological components came into being. At the molecular and biochemical level, biological functions such as vision, blood clotting, self-healing, growth, and basic cell functions have a complexity that exceeds some of mankind's most ingenious creations—such as rocket ships and nuclear power facilities. With current technology, we have no way of explaining how the building-block components of protons, neutrons, and electrons could organize themselves into such incredibly complex living structures unless we assume that some creative being caused this to occur.

For more information about the biochemical issues surrounding evolution, please read the book *Darwin's Black Box* by Michael J. Behe. It is written from a purely scientific perspective, and it analyzes in great detail the biochemical infrastructure of many of the biological building blocks of our world. He explains that the simplest life forms, cells, have irreducible complexity that cannot develop progressively over time in a Darwinian fashion.

I continue to be amazed that many of the more well-educated people of our day adamantly believe in natural evolution and think that any notion of a creator is absurd. In 2015, I heard a scientist on a Saturday afternoon radio broadcast from National Public Radio (NPR) state that if you found a table covered with about 500 pennies and all of the pennies were showing heads, it would be essentially impossible for those pennies to be in that state without some intelligent being or machine organizing them that way. He further stated that a person could bounce that table continually for about a million years before all 500 pennies would again become all heads or all tails. Nonetheless, many well-educated people want to extrapolate ten trillion times further than this to believe that the world and everything in it came together by pure chance and randomness.

However, when it comes to explaining the complexity, precision organization, and origins of our universe, evolutionists unconsciously—or perhaps consciously—believe that creation wished or even willed itself into existence, along the lines of:

- I wish there was a universe or I command a universe to explode from nothing into existence. Of course, in this case the I equates to nothing.
- This nothingness then went further and wished there were the following:
    o Stars, planets, and moons.

ETERNITY

- o At least one planet where life can evolve into plants and animals.
- o Plants that can wish they had the ability to process soil, water, sunlight, and warmth and produce beautiful fragrant flowers.
- Then this nothingness wished there were animals who can wish they had the following:
  - o A genie to make wishes come true
  - o A brain, so they can think of stuff to wish for
  - o A heart
  - o Blood vessels
  - o A nervous system
  - o Bones
  - o Skin
  - o Ability to heal themselves
  - o Lungs
  - o A digestive system
  - o Eye sight
  - o Hearing
  - o Ability to breath
  - o Ability to eat and drink
  - o Ability to speak and even sing
  - o Ability to dream
  - o Ability to sleep
  - o Ability to design things
  - o Ability to walk
  - o Ability to run
  - o Ability to throw
  - o Ability to love
  - o Ability to be loved
  - o Ability to attract the opposite sex
  - o Ability to reproduce
  - o Ability to be funny

Is There A Creator/God?

The following excerpt is from the book *One Second After You... Die* by Mark Cahill, which gives further insights about the complexity and order of our world:

> Every time you see a creation, like a building, you know there is a creator. Every time that you see design, like a cell phone, you know there is a designer. Every time you see art, like a painting, you know there is an artist. Every time you see order, like 20 plates in a row, you know there was an orderer. If you look around the universe, what do you see? You see creation, design, art, and order. If every other thing has a creator, designer, artist, and an orderer behind it, does it not make sense to think there is a Creator, Designer, Artist, and Orderer behind this universe? If you look at the complexity and precise nature of the universe, it just boggles the mind.

The Earth

"The Earth... its size is perfect. The Earth's size and corresponding gravity holds a thin layer of mostly nitrogen and oxygen gases [that only extend] about 50 miles above the Earth's surface. If Earth were smaller, an atmosphere would be impossible, like the planet Mercury. If Earth were larger, its atmosphere would contain free hydrogen, like Jupiter. Earth is the only known planet equipped with an atmosphere of the right mixture of gases to sustain plant, animal, and human life.

The Earth is located the right distance from the sun. Consider the temperature swings we encounter, roughly -30 degrees to +120 degrees [Fahrenheit]. If the Earth were any further away from the sun, we would all freeze. Any closer, and we would burn up. Even a fractional variance in the Earth's position to the sun would make life on Earth impossible. The Earth remains this perfect distance from the sun while it rotates around the sun at a speed of nearly 67,000 mph (miles per hour). It is also rotating on its axis, allowing the entire surface of the Earth to be properly warmed and cooled every day.

And our moon is the perfect size and distance from the Earth for its gravitational pull. The moon creates important ocean tides and movement so ocean waters do not stagnate, and yet our massive oceans are restrained from spilling over across the continents."

Water

"Water... colorless, odorless, and without taste, and yet no living thing can survive without it. Plants, animals, and human beings consist mostly of water (about two-thirds of the human body is water)... the characteristics of water are uniquely suited to life: It has an unusually high boiling point and freezing point. Water allows fluctuating temperature changes, while keeping our bodies a steady 98.6 degrees. Water is also chemically neutral. Without affecting the makeup of the substances it carries, water enables food, medicines, and minerals to be absorbed and used by the body.

Water has a unique surface tension. Water in plants can therefore flow upward against gravity, bringing life-giving water and nutrients to the top of even the tallest trees. Water freezes from the top down and floats, so fish can live in the winter. Ninety-seven percent of the Earth's water is in the oceans. But on our Earth, there is a system designed which removes salt from the water and then distributes that water throughout the globe. Evaporation and people. It is a system of purification and supply that sustains life on this planet, a system of recycled and reused water.

The Brain

"The Human *Brain*... simultaneously processes an amazing amount of information. Your brain takes in all the colors and objects you see, the temperature around you, the pressure of your feet against the floor, the sounds around you, the dryness of your mouth, even the texture of your [computer] keyboard. Your brain holds and processes all your emotions, thoughts, and memories. At the same time, your brain keeps track of the ongoing functions of your body like your breathing pattern, eyelid movement, hunger, and movement of the muscles in your hands.

The human brain processes more than a million messages a second. Your brain weighs the importance of all this data, filtering out the relatively unimportant. This screening function is what allows you to focus and operate effectively in your world. The brain functions differently than other organs. There is an intelligence to it, the ability to reason, to produce feelings, to dream and plan, to take action, and relate to other people."

The Eye

"The human eye is enormously complicated—a perfect and interrelated system of about 40 individual subsystems including the retina, pupil, iris, cornea, lens, and optic nerve. For instance, the retina has approximately 137 million special cells that respond to light and send messages. The retina cells receive light impressions, which are translated to electric pulses and sent to the brain via the optic nerve. A special section of the brain called the visual cortex interprets the pulses to color, contrast, depth, etc., which allows us to see "pictures" of our world. Incredibly, the eye, optic nerve and visual cortex are totally separate and distinct subsystems. Yet together, they capture, deliver and interpret up to 1. 5 million pulse messages a millisecond! It would take dozens of supercomputers programmed perfectly and operating together flawlessly to even get close to performing this task."

I could include many other details about the complexity in our universe, but I will instead stop and ask the evolutionists to answer some tough questions. While I could easily ask thousands of question, I'm willing to entertain any valid evidence to just a few key questions.

- How could natural evolution:
    - Produce eye sight?
    - Produce the individual and complex organs of the human body, such as the heart, the

brain, the digestive system, and the nervous system?
- o Produce seeds that know how to convert themselves via water, soil, and sunlight into a particular species of a tree that produces colored fruit at a certain time of year?
- o Produce a brain capable of handling the processes of sight, sound, smell, touch, and taste?
- o A male species and a female species whereby no additional offspring could be produced without both sexes?
- o Produce dreams in our minds when we go to sleep at night?
- And if natural evolution has, according to most scientists of our day, taken about thirteen billion years to bring us from nothing to what we call the year 2018, explain how the first male and first female of each species happened to be randomly formed in close enough timeline and physical proximity to

each other to be able to mate so that more of their species could exist?
- If our seven billion people cannot yet create the simplest of life forms, how can we fathom that pure random processes will eventually figure out how to form complex living creatures without any involvement with an existing creative intelligent being?
- And my favorite question which is slightly subjective:
    o Why is the world so beautiful and so colorful with its combination of rainbows, blue skies, green plants, white snow, orange and purple flowers, along with spectacular colorful sunsets and golden moonrises?

It seems to me that it takes far more faith to believe in natural evolution. I could expand further on the merits and concerns with the natural evolution theory, but I will instead move on to the subject of creation.

Note

If you check scientific literature from the 1980s, evolutionists had believed the world was just five billion years old. Maybe they should update their theory—or wish—to say that it took a few trillion years to make an impossible fairy tale somewhat believable.

The Bible's Account of Creation

The Bible begins with the account of creation in Genesis, Chapter 1:

Genesis 1:1–31
1. In the beginning God created the heavens and the earth.
2. Now the earth was formless and empty, darkness was over the surface of the deep, and the Spirit of God was hovering over the waters.
3. And God said, "Let there be light," and there was light.

Is There A Creator/God?

4. God saw that the light was good, and he separated the light from the darkness.
5. God called the light "day," and the darkness he called "night." And there was evening, and there was morning—the first day.
6. And God said, "Let there be a vault between the waters to separate water from water."
7. So God made the vault and separated the water under the vault from the water above it. And it was so.
8. God called the vault "sky." And there was evening, and there was morning—the second day.
9. And God said, "Let the water under the sky be gathered to one place, and let dry ground appear." And it was so.
10. God called the dry ground "land," and the gathered waters he called "seas." And God saw that it was good.
11. Then God said, "Let the land produce vegetation: seed-bearing plants and trees on the land that bear fruit with seed in it, according to their various kinds." And it was so.

12. The land produced vegetation: plants bearing seed according to their kinds and trees bearing fruit with seed in it according to their kinds. And God saw that it was good.
13. And there was evening, and there was morning—the third day.
14. And God said, "Let there be lights in the vault of the sky to separate the day from the night, and let them serve as signs to mark sacred times, and days and years,
15. and let them be lights in the vault of the sky to give light on the earth." And it was so.
16. God made two great lights—the greater light to govern the day and the lesser light to govern the night. He also made the stars.
17. God set them in the vault of the sky to give light on the earth,
18. to govern the day and the night, and to separate light from darkness. And God saw that it was good.
19. And there was evening, and there was morning—the fourth day.

20. And God said, "Let the water teem with living creatures, and let birds fly above the earth across the vault of the sky."
21. So God created the great creatures of the sea and every living thing with which the water teems and that moves about in it, according to their kinds, and every winged bird according to its kind. And God saw that it was good.
22. God blessed them and said, "Be fruitful and increase in number and fill the water in the seas, and let the birds increase on the earth."
23. And there was evening, and there was morning—the fifth day.
24. And God said, "Let the land produce living creatures according to their kinds: the livestock, the creatures that move along the ground, and the wild animals, each according to its kind." And it was so.
25. God made the wild animals according to their kinds, the livestock according to their kinds, and all the creatures that move along the ground according to their kinds. And God saw that it was good.

26. Then God said, "Let us make mankind in our image, in our likeness, so that they may rule over the fish in the sea and the birds in the sky, over the livestock and all the wild animals, and over all the creatures that move along the ground."
27. So God created mankind in his own image, in the image of God he created them; male and female he created them.
28. God blessed them and said to them, "Be fruitful and increase in number; fill the earth and subdue it. Rule over the fish in the sea and the birds in the sky and over every living creature that moves on the ground."
29. Then God said, "I give you every seed-bearing plant on the face of the whole earth and every tree that has fruit with seed in it. They will be yours for food.
30. And to all the beasts of the earth and all the birds in the sky and all the creatures that move along the ground—everything that has the breath of life in it—I give every green plant for food." And it was so.

31. God saw all that he had made, and it was very good. And there was evening, and there was morning—the sixth day.

The Bible covers additional aspects of the world's creation over the next eight chapters of Genesis, but the fundamental creation story is complete at the end of Genesis, Chapter 1. The story of creation is mostly covered within the first nine chapters of the Bible. This account of creation was written by a man named Moses more than 3,500 years ago. In Genesis, Chapters 6 through 9, a man named Noah was instructed by God to build a giant boat and house two of every land-dwelling creature in order to preserve their species from an impending global flood. After the flood, Noah, his family, and the surviving animals reinhabited the earth.

While I trust the Genesis account of creation, in light of the world-wide flood of Noah, I cannot easily explain certain mysteries such as how the world survived without ever having rainfall until the time of Noah and how carnivorous animals were originally designed to be vegetarians. Nonetheless, I do believe that the Bible's account of creation has phenomenally greater potential for explaining our world's origins than any theories on evolution. Since current technology and scientific research leave evolutionary theories more in the realm of fairy tales, are we more obligated to believe in the Bible than people of prior generations?

I have heard it expressed that believing in evolution's explanation of the incredible orderliness of our world is about like believing that a dictionary could come from an explosion at a book publishing plant. Likewise, when the World Trade Towers were brought down by terrorists in 2001, it produced a pile of smoldering rubble rather than a new more advanced building. So how can evolutionists believe that an explosion that started the universe—entirely through random chance—form complex entities such as stars that flame for billions of years without being consumed or a planet like earth with a perfect mix of chemicals and materials producing oxygen, water, plants, animals, fuels, metals, wood, atmosphere, and even the hot liquid core of the earth itself?

Is There A Creator/God?

So then why do we live in a society that suppresses creation theories while promoting the far-fetched evolutionary theory as the absolute truth for explaining our world's origins?

There are many theories to try to explain this phenomenon, but in my opinion, the reason why many believe there is no god and/or creator is because of what I refer to as the rivalry syndrome. In general, the idea of rivalry is based on the concept that most people align themselves with some group of people, whether they realize it or not. By default, as people grow from children into adulthood, they generally align with people of similar types and against people who are mocked or ridiculed—unless they have some strong reason to stand with the group of people being mocked. For instance, the United States has two major political parties. These parties are so divided that people who align with one party often feel that any ideas proposed by the other party are bad or wrong. People feel threatened by each other when their political parties become extreme rivals.

Likewise, in the United States today, being an outspoken Christian person is not popular for a variety of reasons. Nonetheless, those who are not Christians typically believe that, if Christians are wrong about certain important matters in life, by extrapolation they must be wrong about all important matters regarding life, death, and even our world's origins—even if their own belief has no solid evidence to support itself. They believe that the truth must be generally opposite of what their rivals believe.

Nonetheless, from the evidence we have today, the statistical likelihood that our world was created by an intelligent being or beings is at least 99.999% and the likelihood that our world came together by pure natural evolution is less than 0.001%. So, are you actually willing to bet your eternity on those odds?

If you question these statistics, search the library or the Internet for yourself and try to find any scientist who can provide reasonable evidence that our world came together by natural evolution without any involvement from a creative being. What you

Is There A Creator/God?

will find instead is that the scientists who are willing to address this debate honestly are scientists who agree that it's statistically impossible for even the most fundamental life form to have come together by pure chance and evolutionary processes.

In this day and time, we have the privilege of having access to far more information on the subject of our world's origins than generations of the past had ever dreamed of. Although it is unlikely that we will ever bring closure to the subject of our world's true origins, I believe that, when we obtain more information in the decades to come, we may find that there is more to the world's fundamental chemical and biological building blocks than just protons, neutrons, electrons, and biological cell formations. Nevertheless, the scientific data we have today greatly favors creation over evolution.

Someone once asked me where God came from. This is an interesting question and one that we may never know the answer to. In fact, this may be the only question that even God does not know the answer to. As long as anything exists, there inherently will be at least one question that can never be answered. Nonetheless, if you're reading this, you also exist, and you had no choice about coming into existence. Someday, your life on this earth will terminate and you'll have no choice about that.

Summary

As I stated at the beginning of this chapter, I did not intend to conclude that science tells us that there is or that there is not a god. Instead, I wanted to present credibility to the idea that some creative being put our world together in case you—the reader—were convinced that natural evolution is the only sufficient and reasonable explanation for our origins. While there exists scientifically based evidence that seems to indicate that certain biological and geological formations are millions or billions of years old, perhaps our creator wants to leave some room for us to believe in the Bible based on other factors, many of which I will address as we go forward.

Remember, it is estimated that there have been about one to two hundred generations on our planet already. Only the most recent generations have lived and died when there was any scientific insight into these matters. There must, therefore, be more to our story than just what science can or cannot tell us. As we begin to analyze the Bible more closely, I hope that you will find great confidence that the Bible is in fact our creator's special book to mankind and that it is reliable about both our creation and the eternity that awaits each of us.

Chapter 2

Who Is This Creator/God?

*N*ow that we have determined that some creative god-like force exists--or existed--to put the world together—although you may still be still skeptical—who is this being or who are these beings who created the universe and everything in it? What would it take for you to believe that there really is a god and that he has communicated to mankind?

If you heard a voice or some being came to you claiming to be the creator of the world, what requests might you make of this being before you would believe? If they could dry up an ocean in front of your eyes, predict events before they happened, give site to blind people, and tell you things about

Who Is This Creator/God?

yourself that only you knew, would you believe? How would you then pass on your belief to others?

The Bible tells about a creator who came to millions of people throughout history and was successful at accomplishing such miracles as mentioned. Some ancient predictions have even come true during this century, such as Israel becoming a nation again after thousands of years of being scattered across the globe.

However, before we go any further, let us address the issue of how we can be sure of any historical events outside the realm of our own personal experiences during our own lifetime. For instance, when the first Apollo missions to the moon were shown on television back in the 1960s, some people thought they were all a hoax. In our present day, however, with satellites flying through space to support weather reporting and global communications, we can trust that the trips to the moon actually happened.

Likewise, we can safely trust that places like Egypt and Japan exist, although many who read this book—myself included—have never been to either of these countries. There is sufficient evidence for us to believe such places exist, including maps, books, food, and people we meet who are from these countries. The Bible, therefore, also can be considered trustworthy regarding the events and people it speaks of just as we trust there is such a place as New York City, because we have archaeological information and written sources from all over the world that validate many of the events of and places referred to in the Bible. We also have people alive today who are descendants of biblical characters. Technically, we are all descendants of Adam, and then again, we all trace back as descendants of Noah. Therefore, we are all cousins and blood relatives to each other.

Trustworthiness of the Bible

Further insights about how believable the Bible is are found in another excerpt from the book *One Second After You ... Die* by Mark Cahill. Keep in mind that this excerpt is based upon biblical passages that you may not be familiar with. However, you can be assured that these amazing claims of fulfilled prophesies have been verified and that you can verify these as well.

Fulfilled Prophecies

The one thing that stood out the most when I was trying to see if the Bible was truthfully God's word was fulfilled prophecies. The basic definition of a prophecy is something said today or in the past that predicts something in the future. Anyone can prophesy anything. We see that with magazines at the checkout counter in the grocery store all the time. The key though is whether you can get your prophecy correct! That is what sets apart a false prophet from a real one.

... Not only did the Bible have hundreds of very, very detailed prophecies in it, they came true!...

There are prophecies in the Bible about certain people, nations, the end times, etc. But some of the most fascinating ones have to do with who the coming Messiah would be. It gave very specific details on who that person is. The Old Testament has over 60 prophecies and 300 references, so you wouldn't need luck or chance to figure out who this person is, but you could know with 100% accuracy!

The Bible says the Messiah (another name for Jesus Christ who is God almighty and who became a person and lived thirty-three years on earth) would be a descendent of King David (who became famous as a boy for fighting the giant called Goliath), born in the very small town of Bethlehem... He would also be born of a virgin... This Messiah would arrive while the Temple was still standing in Jerusalem... The Old Testament says the Messiah would perform miracles, ride into Jerusalem on a donkey, and be betrayed by a friend. He would be sold for thirty pieces of silver and pierced in His hands and feet. Along with all of these prophecies, it also says in the Old Testament that this Messiah would rise from the dead!

Those are some very detailed prophecies! These aren't general predictions like you see in horoscopes or from Nostradamus; but very, very specific accounts. Either God can get all of these correct, or this book is not reliable. And yet to have 100% accuracy, all of these prophecies have come true in the birth, life, death and resurrection of a man called Jesus Christ!

Can you imagine someone predicting all of these right now to happen in some person in 3000 AD? It is almost ludicrous to think about, but that is what has happened here.

ETERNITY

A man named Professor Peter Stoner figured out that the chance of one man fulfilling just eight of those prophecies was 10 to the 17th power. Professor Stoner gave this illustration to explain it:

"If you mark one of ten tickets, and place all the tickets in a hat, and thoroughly stir them, and then ask a blindfolded man to draw one, his chance of getting the right ticket is one in ten. Suppose that we take 10^{17} silver dollars and lay them on the face of Texas. They'll cover all of the state two feet deep. Now mark one of these silver dollars and stir the whole mass thoroughly, all over the state. Blindfold a man and tell him that he can travel as far as he wishes, but he must pick up one silver dollar and say that this is the right one. What chance would he have of getting the right one? Just the same chance that the prophets would've had of writing these eight prophecies and having them all come true in any one man, from their day to the present time, providing they wrote in their own wisdom."

Once again, the statistical likelihood that the Bible is trustworthy is overwhelming. Many people— myself included— believe that we are getting close to the end of the world as we know it. The world has changed dramatically in the last century, where one individual can now cause massive destruction, people can travel across the globe in under a day, and we can communicate in real time with multiple people at any place on the planet. Also, Middle-Eastern nations of old, such as Egypt and other Arab nations, have risen from relative obscurity to become critical players on the global front in the latter part of the 20th century. These nations are the geographic holders of the modern world's economic lifeblood and, unfortunately, the base for the world's most volatile and militant religious groups.

The changes in the world during this century should cause us to have an easier time believing in the Bible than people from any other time, since much of the old predictions of the world have fallen perfectly into place, especially with the incredibly unlikely event of Israel returning to a nation after almost 1,900 years. Most of us in American society are aware of many biblical predictions, even if we have never read the Bible. Various popular movies, books, and television shows have accurately quoted Bible passages about the end times, although their speculation of how the events will take place are not very much in line with what the Bible actually describes.

As I briefly touched on earlier in this book, the final book of the Bible, Revelation, Chapter 9, Verses 7–10, seems to describe the final wars of the world being fought with flying fighting machines described as "locusts... with the faces of men." How could the book's writer nearly 2,000 years ago know that someday airplanes and helicopters would exist and be used in warfare? Nevertheless, you would expect people more than ever to search the Bible for answers, since it has proven to be such a great source of truth. Surprisingly, the Bible seems to be the last place a lot of people are willing to search. This mysterious concept of why people resist the Bible will be discussed as we continue through this book, but it again ties into what I referred to earlier as the rivalry syndrome.

Now that we have briefly considered the Bible's account of a creator communicating to people and how believable these accounts are, I will go into even more detail about the Bible's overall credibility. I have become convinced that the Bible is true and that it indicates that the creative being(s) of the earth consist of just one god. Going forward, I will refer to him as God whenever I am speaking of him specifically. This God, who created the universe and everything in it, exists in spirit throughout the entirety of the universe, and he knows where each molecule is and where it will be at every moment in time. He also knows everything that will happen, when it will happen, and how it will happen. He has no beginning and no ending. This God, however, also exists as a subset of himself in two separate beings—one that is physical and the other that is spiritual. God—the overall creator—refers to himself as the Father, and he refers to his physical entity as the Son. The spiritual entity is referred to as the Holy Spirit.

While God's existence as three entities may be difficult for people to understand, consider that you have a physical body and a soul or spirit held inside you. Many people—even those who doubt the existence of God—believe deep down that there is a part of them that is different from their physical body and that this spirit will survive in some form after their death. When we have our hair cut or our nails trimmed, we don't separate a part of our soul. Also, as humans, we have different roles. A man can be a father to his children, a son to his parents, and a friend or advisor to other people. Thus, it is not surprising that God also has different roles and different components. Nonetheless, trying to simplify God and His entities with such an analogy cannot come close to grasping the awesomeness of this God and His mystery and complexity.

God the Father has not only the power to create and manage the universe, sun, moon, earth, plants, and animals, but He also has the power to know everything that will happen in exact detail. He is never surprised by a weather event, a disease, a mosquito bite, an act of kindness, or an act of evil. However, the Bible indicates that God the Son does not know every detail about events that will happen. While the Son knows much about many things and events that will happen, He may not always know when good events will occur. This may be part of the reason that God the Son especially celebrates happy events.

The Holy Spirit is a special entity who dwells within the Son and who also can dwell in people at specific times and in certain situations. The Bible is not clear as to whether the Holy Spirit is all knowing.

Remember, the creator of our world is one God, though He exists as three entities. What He sees or is capable of knowing may seem confusing. As analogies, consider our experiences with movies or sports. If we have only seen a movie's trailer, we may generally know the basic story of the movie we're about to watch, and we may even know how it will likely turn out. Nevertheless, we still watch the movie because it can take us through a journey that can be thrilling and stir our deepest emotions. If we are watching a live sporting event that we are very interested in, a good match also can take us through an exhilarating adventure. Likewise, God the Son may have seen the trailer or have been given insights about what to expect by God the Father. Nonetheless, the drama and twists and turns of our lives can be thrilling to Jesus as He looks on, watching over and protecting us throughout our life.

To take this further, many of us will watch the same movie more than once or we replay a sporting event that we have already seen. Somehow, we can endure the emotional highs and lows over and over again—even when we know what will happen. Similarly, God the Father can be emotionally impacted by the things that happen—even though He knows what will happen beforehand.

One of my all-time favorite movies is *The Grinch*, staring Jim Carey. I remember that I didn't like the movie trailer and had no interest in seeing it. Nonetheless, we rented it one year around Christmas, and I sat down with the family to watch it. Despite having very low expectations that I would like it, I ended up really enjoying the movie and probably have watched it more than a dozen times since. There are funny parts in that movie that I still laugh at. In fact, I sometimes laugh even harder than the first time I watched it. Ultimately, the part near the end of the movie where the little girl goes to visit the Grinch on Christmas morning—even after the Grinch had done a horrible thing by stealing everyone's Christmas presents—somehow always melts my heart when she tells him that she came to visit because, "No one should be alone on Christmas." This rare act of love and kindness always gets me teary eyed—no matter how many times I watch it. This also gives me confidence that when we are kind towards God or towards people, it melts God's heart even if He knows it's about to happen. This may especially melt Jesus' heart because even He may not know that it's coming.

According to Psalm 139, God wrote the script of our lives long before He created the first human beings on this earth, and God knew at this time that you would be reading this line of this book today—at this moment in your life—at this moment in time. So, if God the Father has already written the script for our life, why are we held accountable and judged (potentially banished to hell forever) for our decisions and actions? That is a mystery that we may never understand until we reach eternity. Nevertheless, we are totally accountable for whether or not we believe in God, whether we love or hate God, and whether we love or hate people.

Summary

If we reconcile ourselves to God, He will send challenges our way. We understand that parents will send their children to school when they reach a certain age. Likewise, we should expect that God will give us assignments and responsibilities as we go through our life. However, if we are close to God, the daily grind of life can be much easier to bear and the challenges placed before us can be enjoyable and exhilarating. Just as children in a happy family are excited to go on adventures with their family, so too can we can be excited about the next chapter of the journey that God has in store for us. Many of us thrive on movies and books about people who've overcome hardships and challenges, but often we don't want any drama in our own life. By recognizing that God has a plan for us all, I hope you'll now be more in tune with the journey of your life and cherish each step as God takes your life forward.

Note

As this book continues, I will refer to God with upper case pronouns, such as He or Himself out of honor and respect to the being who I believe created our entire universe and everything in it. I don't intend to offend females by referring to God with male pronouns, but the Bible does seem to indicate that God aligns Himself as specifically being male.

Chapter 3

Why Were We Created?

So why did God create us? Just as most people desire to have special relationships in their life to fill the void of loneliness, whether it be friends, pets, a spouse, children, or even toys, so too God chose to create a similar environment for Himself.

Angelic Beings

The Bible indicates God first created spiritual beings called angels, whom he gave an environment called heaven that they could inhabit with Him. These beings were given free will to do according to their own desires, not as pre-programmed robots or instinct-based animals. God loved these beings and hoped that they would choose to love Him in turn and establish special friendships with Him and with one another. The Bible isn't clear about how many angelic beings there are, but some passages indicate that there are millions or even billions of them and that they do not procreate or die. The book of Revelation, Chapter 5, Verse 11, mentions that 10,000 times 10,000 angels were before God. In doing the math, this comes to 100 million angels.

By the way, the Bible strongly indicates that all angels are male and that people do not become angels—as many popular movies and television shows like to portray. While angels live in a world that is both spiritual and physical, angels can and have appeared at times in human form. On the other hand, while human beings live in a world with only four dimensions (including the dimension of time), there seem to be other dimensions that we cannot see, touch, hear, or smell. Think of fish in a lighted fish tank in a dark room. They may not be able to see us looking at them through the glass of the aquarium they swim in. Likewise, we cannot normally perceive angelic beings if they

ETERNITY

are near us unless God allows them to enter our personal environment—our aquarium. Angels also appear to have the same general physical appearance of men, as they have at times appeared to and spoken to people, but their physical size can actually vary greatly when they encounter humans. In the book of Luke, Chapter 1, Verses 11–20, the angel Gabriel appeared to a man named Zechariah. It seems that Gabriel was about the size of a typical human in that encounter. However, in the Book of 1 Chronicles, Chapter 21, Verse 16, the angel described seems to appear in a form that is hundreds or maybe thousands of feet tall.

After creating the angels, God later created the universe, the earth, the plants, the animals, and a man. The Bible isn't clear on how long it was between the time He created angels and the time He created the earth. It could have been millions of years or just a very short time. The Bible also isn't clear on how long it was between the time that God formed Adam and then formed Eve. It is possible that there may have been days, weeks, or many years before Eve was created.

Why Were We Created?

God may have created this physical world not only for His own desire, but also to give joy to His angelic beings. The Bible's book of Job, Chapter 38, Verse 7, seems to indicate that the angels were excited by God's creation. At some point before, during, or shortly after the creation of the world and mankind, one third of the angelic beings rebelled against God and were cast out of heaven. They are referred to as demons after that point in time with the devil being their leader. The devil (or Satan) was originally called Lucifer and was the most prominent angel in heaven. The Bible isn't clear on exactly why these angels rebelled, but in Isaiah, Chapter 14, Verses 12–14, we are told that Lucifer was vain about his beauty and position and that he wanted to rule heaven.

The Bible also isn't clear on what caused about a third of the remaining angels to also be cast out of heaven, but my personal theory is that the devil and many of the angels were captivated by Eve, the first female, who was unclothed prior to her sin and the fall of mankind. In the Book of Genesis, Chapter 3, Verses 2–5, the devil approached Eve in the form of a serpent and tried to impress her, just as men have been trying to impress females ever since. The devil tempted her to violate God's instructions, causing sin to enter the world and resulting in punishment to the devil, Adam, and Eve. The Bible, however, indicates that this banishment of the devil and the demons was a one-time and irreversible event—in other words, fallen angels cannot be reconciled with God and angels do not continually fall from God's grace.

Note

In this story of the fall of the angels, the devil isn't directly mentioned as the serpent in the Genesis 3:2–5 passages, although most people understand this to be the case. The book of Revelation, Chapter 12, Verse 9, however, does refer to the devil as being the serpent of old.

The Creation of Mankind

God initially had a close special friendship with Adam. God emphasizes in the book of Genesis,

Chapter 1, that mankind was special from every other animal because God created man in His own image. In fact, no other physical creature exhibits signs that it is moral or self-aware besides humans. Morality and self-awareness provide the ability to know right from wrong and good from evil, to employ rational and irrational behavior, and to show concern about life's meaning and life after death. While some animals such as dogs, cats, monkeys, and dolphins seem to exhibit a compassionate side, I don't think it's of great value in this book to debate the moral nuances between humans and them.

For those who still believe that all plants and animals just randomly formed in the size, shape, and structure they possess, doesn't it seem that our views of the perfect being would be radically different from humans? Why is it that every movie or portrayal of alien creatures who are supposedly more advanced than us generally have similar characteristics of humans rather than those of crabs, birds, or other life forms? Also, if aliens are superior to humans, shouldn't their fashion, romantic styles, and sense of humor be far superior as well? Even

ETERNITY

brilliant Hollywood producers like Steven Spielberg align their aliens in the shape of humans—but with the dress code and skin type of a slug. Additionally, I still haven't seen an alien who's likely to get a lot of responses on a typical dating site. The answer to my rhetorical comments and questions is that humans were designed by God in an incredibly optimal way. While creative beings have unlocked amazing technological capabilities over the past millennia, including electricity, medicine, and the ability to fly, I doubt that our creative human minds will ever come up with a significantly better physical design for intelligent beings.

After creating Adam, God realized that Adam needed special friends just as He had. God created Eve to be Adam's special companion, and God ordained monogamous and lifelong marriage between them. He then gave Adam and Eve the ability to create others whom they could love and enjoy along with God. He gave them an ideal environment to live in, called the Garden of Eden—I imagine it would have made Hawaii look third rate by comparison.

Just as God gave the angels free will, He also gave people free will. Whenever there is free will and free choice, it indicates there are good choices and bad choices. Hence, we have the existence of good and evil. God had clearly instructed Adam and Eve about certain choices they were to avoid. As we discussed earlier, the devil then appeared to Eve in the form of a serpent and convinced her to break one of God's instructions. She then convinced Adam to do the same. Neither Adam nor Eve attempted to even discuss the matter with God. This disobedience—similar to that of the demons who had fallen from God's grace—forced God to remove Adam and Eve from His presence and the paradise they lived in. Unlike the devil and the demons, however, God allowed people to be forgiven of their evil behavior if they sincerely asked Him for forgiveness and changed their lives to reflect their true love for God. God's willingness to forgive people is a most important point in the Bible and is the key to where people will spend eternity.

At this point of the story, God's heart was broken as ours might be if our child, spouse, parent, or close friend were to choose to leave us—even though we had great love and concern for them. This brings us to a critical point. We cannot control how others feel about and behave toward us, but we can control ourselves and how we might influence others. Likewise, God does not try to control us, but simply tries to influence us as positively as possible.

Evil Influences

Meanwhile, God allowed the devil and the demons limited ability to have their evil influence on the world in conjunction with the evil and selfishness that people already have potentially within themselves. My personal theory on why God allows the devil and the demons to influence our world is because they are instrumental to the shaping of and fulfillment of the Bible's prophecy about the world's future. The demons play a role in the struggles of humanity, including storms and disease and annoying things like weeds and mosquitos. The demons, however, go far beyond the harm of weeds and such, as their only hope is that they will disrupt God's plans and thereby save themselves from eternal destruction. Evil people have their own individual agendas, but the demons specifically are doing everything they now can to stop God's plans from being fulfilled. Yet, no matter how much their evil influence harms the world, God can allow good things to come from it.

Just imagine what our world would be like today if Hitler had not come along eighty years ago with the intent of destroying all of the Jewish people. I am in no way saying that the harm he caused was good, but rather that his evil intentions ultimately led to the Jewish people having the world's sympathy and compassion that provided the surviving Jews being given their own land after more than 2,000 years. You see, the Jewish people are what we call those people originally from the nation of Israel. So from that evil act came the fulfillment of prophesy. Likewise, as some religious extremists and terrorists today are trying to exterminate Christians, Jews, the nation of Israel, and anyone else who doesn't agree with them, God will ultimately use this evil for the purpose of reaching the hearts of as many people as possible and setting up the future that He has in store for us.

The Ups and Downs of Love

God created us for His pleasure and for our pleasure as well. Life on this earth and our opportunity for eternal life with God is truly a wonderful gift. Thankfully, God loves us more than we can imagine. He gave us the ability to love, and if you have ever been in love with someone or something, just know that the love God has for you is infinitely greater than the love that you and I can have for Him or anyone or anything else. People who are lucky enough to meet someone special and fall mutually in love generally express that phase of falling in love as the most amazing experience in life. Likewise, if you've personally experienced this kind of deep romantic love, you know that it's both the best time of your life and a time where you may not be able to be your normal self. You may find yourself having trouble eating, sleeping, and/or concentrating on work or other priorities because you can't stop thinking about this person and wishing you could always be with them.

In contrast, if you've ever been in a deep romantic love that ended tragically, you know that it is about the most difficult experience in life. That's why most songs are written about the joy of falling in love or the tragedy of love ending. The emotional roller coaster of love and disappointment is the most thrilling part of life. When a person is truly in love, they usually are willing to do almost anything for the sake of the other person. Unfortunately, even if you're lucky enough to enter a marriage where you are both crazy in love with each other, eventually things will happen that will strain that wonderful love that you have, and the honeymoon will subside to some degree.

I have experienced both deep romantic love and extremely painful heartbreak in my life. I have also experienced lengthy periods of major physical illness. I probably spent about a month of each year of the first thirty years of my life in bed with a fever and severe cold symptoms. It's interesting, however, that I really don't remember a lot of details about the physical suffering, but I do remember many of the emotional thrills and disappointments of love like it just happened yesterday. If someone says the word pneumonia, it hardly catches my attention. However, if someone mentions the name of someone I deeply care about or was once close to, it can immediately capture my thoughts and emotions.

For those who have wanted children and have been lucky enough to hold their own new baby in their arms for the first time, this type of love is indescribable. The feeling of holding some tiny new person who is 50% of you is hard to describe in words. I have been fortunate enough to have had that experience twice in my life, being the father of two wonderful daughters.

Another kind of love that people can be passionate about is sports. It is amazing how we can struggle to breathe when we are watching our favorite sports team battle to win a close contest, especially if winning the game will produce a championship trophy or losing the game will end the season in heartbreak. I love sports and I have had moments where a game totally consumed me and the aftermath of winning or losing impacted me emotionally and physically for many hours. I don't exactly know why something as silly as five guys wearing the basketball jersey for a city we didn't even grow up in can impact us so greatly, but I believe it's because deep down, humans like to be associated with winners and winning. Our ego and love for ourselves is another type of love that has an enormous impact on our lives.

While there are various forms of love that are good, some forms of love can be quite harmful. These include the love of money, the love of idols (celebrities, sports figures, etc.), the love or lust for things inappropriate (desiring our friend's spouse), and the love of things that we know are evil and hurtful to others (gossip, slavery, murder, prostitution). We have to be careful about what we love to be sure that the things we're passionate about aren't hurtful to the things we should love the most. If we trust that the God of the universe can provide for us, then we shouldn't feel that we must work extra hours to get ahead at the expense of spending time with our family. Also, if we are struggling financially, but we are willing to spend massive amounts of money to watch our favorite sports teams play ball, our love for sports may be out of balance. In essence, proper love is generally shown when it's given freely to the benefit of others. Improper love often occurs when it's given conditionally, primarily, or exclusively for our own self-indulgence. I'm not saying that we can't take time to enjoy the blessings of life, but we need to periodically assess our heart to recognize where our time and money really go.

To clarify, suppose you're having dinner with a friend and he tells you about two of his other friends. He tells you how the first guy is fun to be with, but that this guy cheats constantly on his wife, frequently complains about how annoying his children are, is rarely appreciative when good things happen to him, and only spends money on himself. He then mentions his other friend who is also fun to be with. This second friend continually does nice things for his wife and kids, frequently offers to help when there is a need, and pays no attention to other women when they hang out. If he tells you that one of his friends is truly a godly person, it's generally inherent that you'll think he's referring to the second friend as the one who's godly. In reality, most people fall in the middle of the two character profiles, but deep down I think we all appreciate having friends who are more godly in nature, especially when we are having a tough time and need someone around who cares about us. As for ourselves, behaving godly isn't that easy.

Summary

Why were we created? The answer is that God wanted to have special loving friendships with beings who could choose whether or not to love Him.

Chapter 4

Why Is the World Full of Problems?

*L*et's continue with the story of the creation of the world, where people have now fallen and separated themselves from God. As Adam and Eve begin to have children, no person will ever again be without selfishness and evil desire until God himself becomes a part of humanity.

In general, I think you will agree that people can be selfish and difficult at times. Some people, however, believe the myth that there are people who are truly good and innocent. Quite a few people believe themselves to be innocent people who have done the best they can to live good lives under the circumstances they have been dealt. Other people feel so guilty about the things they have done that they condemn themselves because they believe they can never be good enough for God. Some people believe that it is possible to never mess up, so they believe there are people who claim to be perfect.

The truth is that no one is perfect, and no one is completely bad. Try to find the little old lady who never hurt anyone, the perfect child, or the cold-blooded killer, and you will undoubtedly discover that the little old lady gossips sometimes or loses her temper over silly things, the perfect child is often impatient and insensitive to the needs of others, and the cold-blooded killer will instinctively react and save a stranger's child who is about to step out into traffic.

I was in a bookstore recently and was sitting near the café area reading a book when I noticed this very old woman going through the trashcan next to me while murmuring horrible curse words. I listened and realized that she was saying that one of the girls working in the café had thrown out her groceries when she bussed her table. The woman was getting very upset about the situation and her murmuring was getting loud enough for everyone around to feel uncomfortable. I could tell she was an angry bitter person, and I was also feeling uncomfortable and was ready for her to leave.

However, I could tell that God wanted me to try to help her. I caught her attention and asked what happened that had her so upset. She told me the story, and I responded that maybe she should look carefully once more around the table where she had been sitting. I told her that I sometimes misplaced things, and I offered to help her look. She calmed down a bit and went back to her table. The groceries were under a chair where they weren't easy to see. When she came back to me, she was a bit relieved that she found them.

Nonetheless, she was still quite frustrated, so I began to just speak to her nicely. The next thing I knew, she had been sitting with me for about 20 minutes and had told me about a lot of her struggles and problems. She seemed to be angry with many people in her life, including her family members. I asked her if there was anything that could happen to make things better with her family members. I also told her that I would pray that the situation with her family would get better. She actually began smiling and asked why I cared. I told her that many people have been nice to my mom over the years since my dad died and that I just wanted to be a friend to her as well. We started talking about matters of eternity and forgiveness and I spoke with her about a book that I was reading that might be helpful to her. I even offered to buy her a copy, but she wouldn't let me. Finally, after about 45 minutes, she smiled and said thanks for taking time to make her feel better, and then she left. I'm not sure what will become of her, but it just shows that even someone so full of hate and anger has a soft side if we just approach them with kindness and patience. I wish I could say that I take time out to do things like this quite often, but I probably miss many opportunities as I hurry through parts of life.

Acceptable Behavior

So, if we are all guilty at times of selfish or sinful behavior, is there a certain amount of it that is acceptable to God? If not, then who can be right with God?

I recall a pastor once assembling cards with the names of famous historical figures, from Hitler to Mother Theresa and asking young people from the audience to come on stage and place the photos of these figures on a wide chart, where the far left end of the chart was for extremely evil people and the far right end was for very good people. He then asked these young helpers to write their own name on a card and place it on the chart where they think they belong. The pastor then asked all of these helpers to then put a vertical line on the chart to indicate who would go to heaven and who would not. It was very interesting to see how they debated as to where the line should go.

In reality, the line that separates those who go to heaven from those who go to hell is a horizontal line far above them all. The critical issue then is to determine who rose above the line in their lifetime and what determines how someone can rise above the line.

You may have heard the expression, "A friend is someone you really know, but you still like them anyway." This statement is very insightful because we all have had some situations when our friends let us down. If you have not experienced this, you will. Likewise, we all eventually let some of our friends down or hurt them. We will eventually let God down too.

Many of us have met people who impressed us greatly when we first met them, but who we no longer consider to be friends. If you overheard a man or woman—let's say in this case it was a man—you admired speaking very negatively and falsely about you or your close friends, would it create a rift in your relationship with this person? I'm betting it would. If you overheard him tell a mutual friend that you are a worthless idiot, could you ever admire them again? If the comment was said about your child, parent, spouse, or best friend, would you still admire him?

Our situation with God is comparable to that of the man who said such hurtful things. Since we have all complained at times about something or someone, does that not hurt God who created all things? How many times would we need to say nice things to redeem ourselves back to God? How many nice things would the man who called us a worthless idiot have to say or do to redeem himself back to us?

If the man who called you a worthless idiot realized that you had overheard what he said about you, but he chose to pretend nothing was ever said and just tried to be extra nice to you, would you ever again really like him the way you once had? Would you confront him and have him explain why he said something so destructive to your friendship? Most people would not. In our home environment, however, where we are all guilty of saying hurtful things about our family members in the heat of tensions, how do we go on? What is that one thing that can make things right again?

Repentance

The only solution to the dilemma of needing to be redeemed to someone (and rise above the theoretical line we brought up earlier) is sincere apology which is also referred to as repentance.

If you had just overheard your friend call you a worthless idiot and soon after heard him apologize to the listeners for saying such a thing and then blamed himself for being upset, would you feel better about him? Probably so.

If you overheard your friend saying that you were really a great person and he was lucky to have you as a friend, would you be able to continue your friendship with them? Probably so. To take this even further, if you overheard someone you greatly disliked saying very nice things to others about you, would you probably start to feel you could actually be friends with that person?

Along with repentance, it is also critical that we understand forgiveness. Up to this point, we have not really thought about our role in the scenario where our friend called us a worthless idiot, and our response to the situation is critical. It is critical to ourselves more so than to the other person.

Let's take another example and assume our eight-year-old child calls us a worthless idiot.

Hopefully, we will have enough love and maturity to give the child a clear understanding of how hurtful saying something like that can be. Some parents in our society might say something very destructive to the child about his own character. Others might develop a dislike and bitterness toward that child. Even if the child had enough insight on his own to apologize, some parents might still have difficulty forgiving.

Now if reality indicates we have difficulty forgiving and dealing with those who really may be too young to understand what they are saying or doing, it is no wonder that we have difficulty forgiving others. The appropriate response to our eight-year-old is to pull them aside, explain to them that what they said hurt us, that they would not appreciate such things being said about them, and that we love them and do not want to see them hurt themselves and others by saying such things. If they respond by telling us they heard us call mom a worthless idiot and that we never apologized to her, then we had better apologize to mom and to our child. If we cannot apologize for our mistakes, we certainly cannot expect our children to do so.

Fortunately for us, God has enough love, character, and integrity to forgive the things people do that hurt Him and those He created. The bad news, however, is that most people will not do their part in the interpersonal relationship process. Remember the three concepts we have been discussing—sin, repentance, and forgiveness—and you will have insight as to what I am getting at. We do fine in the sin part—making mistakes, hurting people, hurting ourselves, being angry and frustrated, and so on. The bigger problem, however, is that we almost always do poorly with apologizing to and forgiving others. In fact, this loving, forgiving God only forgives those who are willing to apologize. In the Book of Matthew, Chapter 6, Verse 12, a passage referred to as the Lord's prayer, it indicates that God forgives us IF we forgive others and AS we forgive others.

I remember when I was about four years old being angry one summer day with my mom because she wouldn't let me do something. It seems she wouldn't let me go with my eight- and eleven-year-old brothers to the ball park. My brothers and their friends were assembling on our front steps when I gave them the news that mom had refused to let me go. I remember telling them that it was stupid that I couldn't go and that I would tell my mom that when she came out with their snacks and drinks. These bigger kids all looked at me like I was just talking smack. So when my mom came out and I told her in front of all these older kids that she was being stupid for not letting me go, she snatched me up like a loaf of bread and took me inside for a spanking.

It seems I remember my brothers telling me later on that their buddies thought I had a lot of guts—but not a lot of brains. Also, looking back on it now as an adult, I know that I would never let a four-year-old child of mine go to the ballpark for an entire afternoon without an adult present, so my mom did the right thing. Instead, I really had been the selfish stupid one in so many ways in this story. I think I ate dinner standing up that evening because sitting in the chair wasn't too enjoyable after a spanking from mom and another later from dad after he got home from work. I don't think I ever really apologized at that time, but I don't think my parents ever loved me less from this incident. I was, however, much more thoughtful, tactful, and respectful from that day forward if I questioned my parents' decisions. In fact, seeing that I never did something quite like that again, in the end, we all thought it was a pretty funny story about the challenges of teaching children to be respectful. However, as we get older, our sinfulness and disrespect can hurt much more deeply. Therefore, it is very important for us to teach our children to apologize when they hurt someone and for us, as adults, to continually grow in our ability to apologize when we hurt others.

When my daughters were really young and wanted to do things they weren't old enough to do, I would sometimes remember this story from my youth and I would ask my girls if they would let their own kids do this if they were in this situation someday. I remember them responding on some occasions with a sudden and emphatic, "No way!" which caused them to immediately retract or alter their request. We would then discuss alternative fun things that we could do and the mini-drama generally turned out well. However, there were also times when I also just said no to my girls without explanation, and those were the times that they weren't very cooperative or happy with my decision.

Love and Forgiveness

Ultimately, there are only three real responses to God regarding our selfishness and sinfulness. Since we have all sinned against or offended God at some point, we can either [1] ask God to forgive us, [2] try to make it up to God by doing good, or [3] convince ourselves into believing the problem is something different than it really is.

Before the fall of some angels and then of people, God had intended to let angels live forever with Him in heaven and let people live forever in paradise on earth. It also seems that he intended for angels to roam the earth at times as well. After the fall, however, God created a place of eternal punishment called hell.

Why Is The World Full Of Problems?

There is nothing I can find in the Bible to indicate that the fallen angels, including the devil, will avoid spending eternity in hell. Also, according to the Bible, all people will—by default—spend eternity in hell unless they die prior to the age of accountability or they have asked God for forgiveness and changed their life to reflect that they love God and all people. This issue is therefore paramount to our eternal destination. By the way, no one knows when this age of accountability occurs exactly, but I believe that anyone mature enough to read and understand the basic issues of this book may have passed this age and is no longer exempt by the ignorance and innocence of youth.

My last point stated that there is this terrible fate that awaits many people, and that likely has your emotions somewhat on edge. Whether you agree with my statements regarding hell or not, please stay with me, as your eternal destiny is at stake. I am sharing my beliefs with you because I know God loves you and cares so much for you. Because God has taught me to truly love and care for people, I want you to know that I also care very much about you. It's also likely that the person who suggested this book to you cares very much about you as well.

Since the Bible is right on every critical issue that we have the ability to examine, there is no reason to believe that the those parts of the Bible about creation, heaven, hell, angels, and demons are not correct, especially when these elements so accurately explain the evil condition of our world today. Although we cannot watch films of God creating the world in six days on the Discovery Channel or get CNN to interview people in heaven or hell, we can verify an enormous amount of facts about the Bible. In addition, we have inherently uncovered the one element that makes the Bible different from any other religious, philosophy, or science book. That element is the Bible's perspective of issues being completely A or B, left or right, and right or wrong.

Only one religious foundational book in the world, the Bible, explains the solution to everyone's problem. A restored relationship with the creator is the only way to true happiness and the only way to spend eternity in heaven and avoid hell. To my knowledge, no other book makes this claim. If the

Bible is right, all the others are wrong. If the Bible is wrong, then maybe some other book is right. We have, however, provided overwhelming evidence that there is a God, that there is sin, and that only repentance and forgiveness restore friendships with people. Therefore, for God to say that the only way to spend eternity in heaven is to restore your relationship with Him, it fits the pattern and makes perfect sense.

However, God takes the matter even further by providing a test that we can truly measure ourselves against. God states that if we hate our brother, then we cannot love God. In the book of Matthew, Chapter 4, Verses 44–48, Jesus tells us, "Love your enemies and pray for those who persecute you." He further states, "Even evil people love those who love them."

God will only let people into heaven who truly love Him. For example, you live in an apartment building and you see riots occurring in the street outside your window. Suddenly, someone is in your hallway, and you hear teenage kids banging on doors for someone to let them in. Would you open the door? If it happened to be a good friend and his kids, would you let them in? I hope so.

Imagine how many problems in this world would be solved if no one truly hated anyone. What if no one was willing to make fun of others? What if no one was intimate with anyone other than with the person they were married to? What if no one was willing to exploit people for their own personal gain? The problems we face would be drastically different, and we could depend on so many people to help us when difficult circumstances would arise. Likewise, so many people could depend on us to help them in various ways.

Restoring Relationships with God

Let us refer back to the three responses to God: [1] ask God to forgive us, [2] try to make it up to God by doing good, or [3] convince ourselves into believing the problem is something different than it really is. Since the devil and demons now hate God and want to stop Him from sending them to hell someday, they spend their entire existence trying to attack God and anything He loves. This is similar to behavior that goes on in human warfare, where both sides try to undermine the other through any methods they can.

The devil knows that God wants people to restore relationships with Him and with each other more than anything else. Therefore, if the devil can do anything to keep those relationships apart, then he will have hurt God the most. The devil hopes this will disrupt God's plans and timing.

The devil also knows that God has written in the Bible that God will fulfill certain prophecies before God casts him and the demons in the lake of fire forever. As a result, the devil is doing everything he can to try to prevent or delay these prophecies from being fulfilled. Therefore, the devil will gladly help people establish false religions that outwardly look good but ultimately do no good because they only sidetrack people into response number 2—redeem yourself with God by doing good rather than through repentance and forgiveness. Likewise, the devil will also use bad things, such as hatred, pride, drugs, money, immorality, greed, war, dissension, and so on to sidetrack people into response number 3—confused into believing the problem is something other than broken relationships with God.

Why does God not just get rid of the devil and the demons? Eventually, He will. For now, this spiritual warfare is one of the aspects of life that we just have to accept. Just as there are 24 hours in a day, crime in the world, and storms we will all face, so too we must deal with God allowing these evil influences to exist. Likewise, just as there are dangerous creatures lurking in the wilderness (lions, tigers, and bears) and dangerous creatures in rivers and the ocean (crocodiles and sharks), so too does our reality face dangerous beings who can harm us without notice. Remember though, about two-thirds of the spiritual beings are still on God's side and are fighting to help protect us and to help us restore relationships with God and with all mankind.

Perhaps that's why God created special animals (dogs, horses, dolphins, etc.) that also help to comfort and protect us from various dangers. Nonetheless, we can all attest that it only takes a small percentage of misguided beings to cause large problems for everyone. One crazy political leader, terrorist, difficult employee, or irate neighbor can create big headaches, even if most every person we know is easy to get along with. Similarly, it's much more comforting to have a pack of loyal dogs with you if you encounter a grizzly bear while walking through the woods. God's angels are willing to work hard to protect us, but they may not be helpful if we enjoy evil and want to walk in darkness. If we insist on swimming alone in dangerous waters or walking through the wilderness unprepared, we are much more likely to create problems for ourselves.

Should God intervene, however, and stop us from doing the wrong things? Should he cause a criminal's car to breakdown so that he cannot victimize the person who he intends to harm? There have been instances where God has intervened in situations like this, but if He did it every time, would He really be allowing us to make our own decisions? I have a friend who is one of the kindest and most gentle persons I've ever known, but he had gotten involved with selling drugs when he was in his late teens. On one particular day, he and his buddy were supposed to pick up a large sum of money and drop off an expensive bundle of drugs, but their car broke down on the way to the meeting place. Later, they found out that the people buying the drugs had intended to kill them both, taking their money and drugs. It turned out that this group of people buying drugs had killed other drug dealers earlier that day and intended to kill my friend and his buddy if they had shown up. That scared my friend so badly that he never had anything to do with drugs after that. He became a Christian when he realized the miracle from God that had saved him that day.

We seldom want to hear that something good can come out of our biggest hardships. In reality, the person who can help us most during our deepest difficulties in life is often someone who went through a similar hardship. I never knew what to say to someone who had a miscarriage until I experienced the loss of my own expectant child. A person who had their heart broken is a person who can help us get through our own broken heart. Additionally, for every painful situation we experience, people who care deeply about us also hurt. Likewise, God hurts greatly when we hurt, but God also feels great joy when we are thankful and joyful that our prayers have been answered. Mr. Rogers Neighborhood was a television show for children that aired in the United States for several decades. The show's lead, Fred Rogers, was one of the most genuinely kind people of our era. He once stated that when he was a child and something tragic happened, his mother would say, "Look at all those people helping."

For many people, their biggest obstacle with believing that God is relevant is that they don't understand why there is so much pain and suffering in the world. They insist that if God was real, that people wouldn't go through such pain and hardships. I heard a few interesting analogies and stories over the years that may help shed light on this difficult subject.

In the first analogy, a man is talking with his barber, and his barber tells him that he doesn't believe that God exists because there are so many people struggling in the world. After the barber's customer pays his bill and leaves the barber shop, he sees a man standing nearby who hasn't had a haircut in many years. He walks this man back into the barber shop and says he no longer believes that barbers exist. The barber laughs and says of course barbers exist. The customer then asks why then that this long-haired man hasn't had a haircut. The barber responds that it's not the barber's fault that the man chooses not to get a haircut. The barber then realizes that it's not God's fault either if people choose not to come to Him.

In a similar vein, I heard a speech recently from Tony Dungy, who's famous for being a great NFL football player and coach. Tony has a son with a rare disorder in his nervous system that causes his son not to feel pain. While this sounds like a gift that most people would love, it actually has been very difficult for Tony, his son, and the rest of his family. Because his son can't feel pain, they found themselves having to go the emergency room continuously for all types of issues. For example, their son could put his hand on the stove and badly burn his hand without even realizing it and they would have to rush to get his damaged hand treated. Also, when his son was really young, he would jump off roofs or playground equipment and break bones and keep going without even realizing that he could cause permanent handicaps if he wasn't treated quickly.

While pain is certainly not enjoyable, God actually gave us a gift by allowing our bodies, our minds, and our hearts to experience pain. Likewise, He gave us the ability to experience great joy and pleasure in our bodies, hearts, and minds when we are in love or when we are in a happy situation. In reality, knowing that we can experience pain can make us much happier and more thankful when we're not experiencing pain. As we discussed in an earlier section, someone who has experienced the pain of losing their parent or who has fought cancer is better able to help another person who just lost their parent or who is fighting cancer.

There are countless other examples where the pain I experienced in the past now allows me to have compassion for others going through similar challenges. There's a powerful old saying, "If you only get sunshine, you'll live in a desert." Most of us relish the beauty of green hillsides covered with spring flowers, but we know that this environment cannot exist without rainy or even stormy days.

While many problems that cause extreme pain and hardship are truly difficult for us to understand—especially at the time we are experiencing them—there are surprisingly good things that can come from difficult situations. I was told something amazing by several people who serve in foreign missions. They said that people who live in countries hostile to the Christian religion—where they could be beaten, jailed or even killed for speaking out about Christ—are more willing to reach out to nonbelievers than we are here in America. Even though the risks to them are much greater, so are the joys of sharing their knowledge.

So where do you stand with God right now? Are there still hurdles between you and God? Many people feel God is not fair to send people to hell forever not reconciling themselves to God. Likewise, many believe it is not fair that criminals can ask for forgiveness before they die and spend forever in heaven. Many argue that if God revealed Himself to everyone, then everybody would repent and be saved, and crime and evil would come to a complete stop. In other words, God should not condemn people if He does not sufficiently inform them of sin, heaven, and hell. People believe that up until now God really has not been doing His fair share of informing us. Some readers may still even doubt there is a God, further indicating that—if He really exists—He is really doing a poor job in marketing Himself.

The real issue is whether people want to know the truth. I believe that anyone reading a book like this is fortunate to have this opportunity. Many people die without having received a lot of written information from God about the meaning of life and salvation. Nevertheless, God has enough ways to pump information about Himself into our lives so that everyone can truly choose to believe or not believe. Just look at the beauty of a spring day with orange, pink, purple and yellow flowers blooming, emerald green grass covering the ground, cobalt blue skies filling the air, and gorgeous spectacular sunsets. God decorated the world around us in such wonder and detail—beyond our comprehension—but we often go through the days and seasons without even noticing. Also, recall how we are wired to know right from wrong and that we can immediately identify ungodly behavior as soon as we see it.

I personally believe that the percentage of people who will be saved is higher in places where efforts are made to distribute information, such as Bibles and books like this. I also believe that when we read books like this, we will be happier and more at peace and able to help make the lives of others more peaceful and happy. Surprisingly, many people from biblical times who witnessed amazing miracles—such as the crossing of the Red Sea, where God parted the waters for the Jews to escape the Egyptians—still could not believe in God, repent, and live by faith. Therefore, God could do amazing miracles for us every day. He could open heaven and talk to us personally every day. Regardless of all that, many of us still would not choose to believe, repent, and trust God—and love everyone.

Summary

This chapter's title indicates that an explanation would be given about why the world has so many problems. The conclusion is that because selfish and evil desires are present in everyone this collectively creates a world full of problems. It is not God's intention for us to live troubled lives on this earth, but many of the problems we face are caused by the sinful actions of mankind. If everyone truly loved God and the other beings He created, the volume and severity of problems that face the world would be drastically reduced.

As long as free choice exists in our current physical reality, there always will be confused people who fight to suppress truth, love, and—most of all—God. This confusion results in a world continually struggling with pain and heartbreak. However, those who love God and whose lives truly reflect that will no longer be able to sin or be a victim of sin once they are in heaven.

Chapter 5:

The Bible: Adam to the Tower of Babel

Our biblical story continues with Adam and Eve giving birth to the first two children on earth, Cain and Abel. When the two were grown, there was a particular situation where Cain became jealous of Abel, and for some reason, Cain killed his brother Abel. There were no prisons at that time, but the Bible states that God put a curse on Cain and banished him from the area where he had grown up. Cain eventually married and had children by a woman who was either his sister or niece.

Adam and Eve had another son, Seth, who had his own children, grandchildren, and so on. According to the book of Luke, Chapter 3, Verses 36–38, there were nine generations from Seth to

Noah. By the time Noah was born, the world was an evil place and Noah was the only person who truly had faith in and love for God. Up until this point, people were living lives up to 900 plus years. After Noah's time, God limited peoples' life span to about 120 years.

While the book of Genesis continues to be very thought provoking to the scientifically inclined, it is also interesting to the relationship minded. God's personal interest in people and having friendships with them is fundamental throughout the Bible. There are also many valuable insights into the basic problems we face today in these important first few chapters of the Bible.

The book of Genesis mentions another interesting story that occurred not long after the flood about the Tower of Babel, which has important implications from a scientific, racial, and cultural standpoint. Instead of people multiplying and filling the earth as God had initially instructed Adam and Eve, people started organizing to build one great city and a tower into the heavens. Since this violated God's instruction for mankind to inhabit the earth, God decided to confuse their language so that they could not understand each other. It is not indicated whether the confusion was done instantly and inflicted haphazardly by families, groups, or individuals. Nevertheless, this language barrier triggered divisions that caused the people to spread out and develop their own villages, cities, nations, and cultures.

God may have at this time also altered some physical attributes of the different groups of people based on the climate he intended them to live in, such as lightening the skin of people who would live in colder, cloudier climates and darkening the skin of people who would live in hotter, sunnier climates. Likewise, God could have allowed these people to adapt over time to their climates, a theory I somewhat believe because of the gradual change that occurs from the skin tone and hair and facial features of cultures and nations as the world is panned from central Africa to northern Europe. Consider the physical attributes of people in these areas: central Africa (very dark skin, very wavy black hair), northern Africa (dark skin, wavy black hair), the Middle East (medium skin, straighter black hair), southern Asia (medium skin, very straight black hair), southern Europe (lighter skin, straighter brown hair), northern Asia (light skin, straight brown hair), northern Europe (very light skin, very straight blond hair)—it becomes apparent that the climate that our ancestors lived in may have played a great role in many of our physical attributes.

As for natives of the western hemisphere, who are a bit darker than expected for the climate of the Americas, the old theory of northeastern Asians migrating across land bridges between Russia and Alaska makes sense when the physical attributes are considered. Native North and South Americans are a very close physical matched to central Asians and Northern Asians.

Now the evolutionists may claim that I agree with them on natural adaptation based on the ideas I just proposed, but I believe that God—not nature—chose at times to alter people's characteristics to help them better survive. The more we learn about genetics, the more we understand that DNA has many switches that—when activated—affect many types of physical attributes, including height, skin tone, and even adaptability to heat and cold. Some scientific writings claim this further supports evolution, but I believe it just shows how smart God was when he designed the human body. As we discussed in Chapter 1, science cannot come close to explaining how DNA itself could have ever developed in a natural evolutionary way, so DNA switching further confirms that an extremely intelligent being designed and created the human body and all its complex building blocks. For those still believing that evolution explains our origins, even though we've considered that it's statistically beyond impossible, here is an analogy to consider. As I stated earlier, believing in natural evolution is comparable to believing that a dictionary could result from an explosion at a printing press. If you still believe this world exists without an intelligent creator(s) having formulated this universe with all of the incredible order of our world and our biology, I can only pray that God will someday soon remove the blinders and allow you to see what even young children consider obvious.

When I was a young child, I was told, like most kids growing up in America, that when we lose a tooth, we should put it under our pillow before we go to bed because the Tooth Fairy would find it. We would wake to find the tooth missing and money in its place. My friends and I may not have been the brightest bunch in the world, but we all knew by six or seven years old that there was no logical way to explain how the Tooth Fairy could find all of the teeth each night for all the children in America. We knew it was just mom and dad having fun with us. So why can't highly educated adults see that a universe occurring apart from a creative intelligent source is impossible and unthinkable? Again, as I stated earlier, it goes back in a significant way to the rivalry syndrome in combination with our own free will that drive us to feel that anything that our enemies (or rivals) believe must be wrong and the truth must be something quite different or even completely opposite to their beliefs.

As I thought of the analogy of the Tooth Fairy as I was writing this part of the book, a few other humorous insights came to mind. I grew up in the south, where the men in my family hunted a lot and kept plenty of rifles, shotguns, and ammo hanging on the den wall. If some strange fairy guy was entering our home every night and looking under the pillows of the children, this fairy would have been shot or arrested a long time ago. Similarly, those touting this theory of evolution and forcing our kids to be taught that it's absolute truth and that any other ideas are a fantasy, will someday be apprehended by God and stand in judgment if they don't wake up while on this side of eternity. As I've said before, I am open to discussion to anyone who believes in evolution and who can actually bring any reasonable evidence to support it. Please start with my list of basic questions in Chapter 1.

Regarding our discussion about the formation of the human races, *The Answers Book* by authors and scientists Ken Hamm, Andrew Snelling, and Carl Wieland is a book I highly recommend everyone to read, especially those who want to know more about creation and evolution. In this book, they give very solid information supporting these principles of creationism, and they have detailed scientific insights about the racial differences that have developed.

Here are a few of their astute perceptions about physical differences among human races. Skin tone and eye color are simply an issue of the amount of melanin a person has (there is no such thing as skin colors but only skin tone). As the world became divided, possibly by the confusion surrounding the Tower of Babel, the spreading out of people could have caused those with more melanin, hence darker skin, to feel more comfortable in warmer, sunnier climates because more sunlight is required to supply vitamin D to a person with higher melanin levels. Likewise, as people with higher melanin levels located to more suitable locations, then there would also be more of a tendency for people with darker skin to intermarry.

On the other hand, people with lesser amounts of melanin tend to sunburn and get skin irritations, so there would have been a tendency for them to seek cooler, cloudier climates. As for the Eskimos, who have fairly dark skin, they may have lived in the colder climates for the sake of survival and just to have a place to live. They may have preferred a warmer environment, but social, economic, and political warfare issues may have been a stronger concern.

Summary

I do not have answers to every question about the Bible and creationism—answers which only God knows—but I thought it would be beneficial to discuss some realistic possibilities to questions that can be a major stumbling block to some people. While I have gone into some detail on these theories, the interested person can find even more information from the Suggested Resources and Bibliography at the end of this book or from many local public libraries, churches, or Christian bookstores.

Chapter 6

The Bible: Who Was Abraham?

As we go forth with discussion of Biblical characters, we are going to start getting into some areas about the basis for salvation and controversial doctrinal issues. Be aware that, while the fundamentals for salvation and such are very clear, applying the intricate details of peoples' lives is not always so clear. Some people who the Bible shows as being alive in heaven hundreds of years after their deaths (and they are still alive today in heaven), such as Abraham, Moses, David, and Elijah, were considered great men by God. Each of these people, however, did some things during their life—even at times when they were in very close contact with God—that were pretty bad by even our weak moral standards today. This confuses many people, but the confusion is because most of those confused are not basing their understanding using the foundations of good and evil that we discussed in earlier chapters.

Let's return back to the Bible where a number of centuries and generations have now passed since Noah and the Tower of Babel. The earth again has become a fairly evil place with most people living lives far removed from any knowledge of or love for God.

A man named Abraham, however, caught God's attention. Although Abraham did not have many of the resources to help him understand God the way we now do, he nonetheless was able to recognize enough fundamental principles about right and wrong in the world that he lived in to know that a holy and personal God must exist to have put this world together and have taken care of it in spite of the evil that can occur.

Abraham is probably one of the ten most important persons to have ever lived on this earth, which is a group that includes the number one person, Jesus, and then John the Baptist, Moses, Abraham, Joseph (son of Jacob/Israel), Peter, Paul,

The Bible: Who Was Abraham?

Mary (the mother of Jesus), David, and Noah. I do not know for sure that this is God's top ten list and if this is how God would order it (if He has such a list), but these people certainly played major roles in this world we now live in. Abraham was much different than other people living at his time. While most people had little regard for God, Abraham, who was actually called Abram at the time, did what the whole focus of this book is about. He looked for the answers to the critical matters of life. Because God is always searching for anyone who will seek Him, God helped Abraham find the knowledge, love, and faith that allowed them to establish a friendship, which is God's ultimate goal for all of us.

When Abraham established a friendship with God, God actually became personally involved in his life. At times, God spoke directly to Abraham and even appeared to him in what many people feel was the pre-incarnate form of Jesus. It is my understanding that God really had not directly interacted with anyone in this way since Noah. Although with Noah, the Bible isn't clear on how God communicated with him, but we know that God gave

Noah very clear instructions on how to make the ark, including the full blueprint for its dimensions. Nevertheless, as Abraham tried to understand life and tried to survive the daily struggles we all experience, God played a special role. God promised to give Abraham children, grandchildren, and so on who would be very numerous and special for all mankind. As Abraham got older, he and his wife had no children. This put their relationship with God to the test. If God loved them and felt they were special, why was He letting them be humiliated by having no children—a popular view of the culture at that time. Moreover, how could they have countless grandchildren if they had no children at all?

This very test of time and faithfulness that God put them through was very much part of His plan. Allowing Abraham and his wife Sarah to have children at very old ages certainly was more convincing to them and to others that God was involved in their lives. In fact, they only had one child, making the idea of a significant number of offspring hard to fathom. In fact, while waiting for God to allow them to have children, they finally got impatient and

The Bible: Who Was Abraham?

took matters into their own hands. Sarah thought maybe Abraham was to have these children by someone else because she had gotten too old, so she had one of her servants bear a child by him. This child, Ishmael, is the father of the Arab people. Later, Abraham and Sarah had their own son, Isaac. Isaac would go on to become the father of Esau and Jacob. Jacob would later be named Israel and be the father of the nation of Israel and of the Jewish people. Sadly, but as most people on the globe are aware, the Arab people and Jewish people have been in conflict since the time of Abraham.

It seems that I spend more time explaining the spiritual implications to these quick pieces of historical information that I present, but that is basically the purpose of this book. I want to try to shed some light on these simple—yet somewhat spiritually complex matters—because this insight is significant to understanding God and in helping us establish a real-life friendship with God.

If God had told Abraham and Sarah that they were going to have children, why did they handle the matter their own way instead of trusting that

God would take care of it when the time was right? On the one hand, they showed they believed God by allowing Abraham to have some avenue to fulfill God's will. At that time, having a maid-servant play the role of surrogate mother was legal, so they weren't violating any laws of the land. On the other hand, they violated a more important principle of God's marriage sacrament by allowing an outside relationship. Although the Ten Commandments had not been mandated at this point in history, basic moral ethics, which God says we all have inherent within us, should have prevented them from solving the dilemma this way.

After Abraham and Sarah did this wrongful act, why did God not give up on them and cancel His plans for Abraham? This is another very important matter. Let us first remember that, when it comes to anything special God seems to want to do, the devil and the other demons play a major role in trying to mess things up. Therefore, it is a safe bet that Abraham and Sarah's lives were under greater spiritual attack than most people during his lifetime. Likewise, God probably had angelic forces working to protect them as well. Nonetheless, things turned out the way God ultimately planned, although the demons probably thought that Ishmael would work only to their favor.

Another thing to consider is how much we all are capable of taking matters into our own hands. Every wrong thing we do really is the same fundamental mistake that they made. God tells us that He will take care of us, but we all at some point make the wrong decisions. We act impulsively when we get impatient, feel sick, are hungry, are concerned about finances, have sexual desires, become frustrated by the wrongful actions of others, etc. Most disagreements in life are really over silly, selfish, childish things, but they cause frustrations that can lead to gossip, harsh words, violence, divorce, drug and alcohol abuse, murder, abortion, war, etc. Although what Abraham and Sarah did was ultimately wrong, the fact that God did not give up on them indicates something very good for all of us. If we truly love God on His terms and we do something wrong, we are able to recognize our fault and be grieved over hurting Him. In turn, He is happy to forgive us and to help us.

The key part to this is the love for God that Abraham and Sarah had, indicating their obvious belief in Him, and the ability to be upset for hurting someone they loved. Chances are that both of them were embarrassed and sorry for what they had done. It is my understanding that they apologized to God for it. God did eventually go through with His plan to allow them to have a child. For me and for you, though, the matter of how we stand with God is up to us.

Up to this point, Abraham's story does not seem to be that of a significant world figure. However, it is not the great kings, athletes, or warriors who God finds most significant. Indeed, the Bible states that Abraham and John the Baptist were two of the most significant people to ever walk the earth. Both have life events in common. Abraham had a son at an extremely old age, and John the Baptist was born to parents who were extremely old at the time of his birth. Sometimes God allows us to wait, so when He responds, it will be much more obvious that God had His hand in the situation.

After Abraham finally got his long-awaited son, God did something that seems very irrational and bizarre by our society's values. God asked Abraham to offer Isaac as a sacrifice. This would kill this only son. Nonetheless, Abraham had faith that if God went to the trouble to bring Isaac into this world, that God must have a plan beyond his understanding to either allow Isaac not to die, or to allow Isaac to come back to life if he did die. Abraham was prepared to offer his son as a sacrifice, but just before he went through with it, God called Abraham to hold off. Once God saw that Abraham was willing to do what He had asked, even in the case of sacrificing the most important person in the world to him—his new child—God called off the test.

Summary

- Do I love God?
- Do I really love everyone?
- Am I upset with myself and capable of apologizing when I do something to hurt someone?

In a nutshell, these three questions are the entrance exam for heaven. We better figure out how to make ourselves truly answer yes to each question before our life is over.

The story of Abraham may not be easy to comprehend, but there is incredible information about God and His love for us that we can draw out of it. First, we need to understand that God put us on this earth because He wanted to have very special friendships with us. Likewise, parents should have the same purpose for bringing their own children into this world. Second, we need to recognize that anyone who does not have a relationship with God is in big trouble for eternity unless that person becomes reconciled to God. Third, a person who truly loves God should be willing to help those who are not reconciled to God.

When we get to the story of Jesus and see that He is God's Son and that He was put to death as the means to truly reconcile people back to God, this story of Abraham being willing to sacrifice his own son Isaac will have even more significance.

There are other aspects to Abraham's life that were significant, but we will move on to help further the foundation of what the world is all about. As we've progressed through this book, we also have been proceeding through the Bible in a parallel fashion. We now find ourselves about twenty chapters into the Bible, which is only about 2% of the way through the whole book. But this 2% is foundational to the rest of the Bible and God's written communication to mankind.

Chapter 7

The Bible: Abraham to Moses

Jacob and Esau

Our story now continues where Abraham's son Isaac grows up, marries, and has twin sons named Esau and Jacob. God indicates to Isaac that the younger son is the one who will become blessed, though it is usually the older son who is blessed by the father, where being blessed means being given special privileges, inheritance, etc. as many firstborn are given today. Isaac turned out to be generally a good father, but he favored his older son, Esau. Rebekah, his wife, also turned out to be generally a good mother, but she favored the younger son, Jacob.

This favoritism became a big problem in this family—as it often does with any family today. Instead of the parents concentrating on helping their children establish deep friendships with each other and with God, they got side-tracked into other priorities and concerns for their children. Isaac set his mind on ways to bypass God's will and pass on his blessing to Esau. Rebekah set her mind on finding a trick to get her husband to pass on the blessing to Jacob. Rebekah then conspired with Jacob to trick Isaac into giving Jacob the blessing. Esau became furious when he found out that Jacob had tricked him and stolen his blessing, and Jacob fled to a distant place.

Again, this seems to be shaping up as another bizarre story, but the Bible is real, just as these situations are real to a lot of families even today. In many inheritance matters, there are strong feelings of favoritism, greed, and hurt taking place among the parties involved. Although some religious or story books may make their star characters appear to be perfect, such as in cult books or many of the Disney movies, in reality, everyone has dark secrets that they hope will never be exposed. The Bible tells us the deeper details about many characters who shaped the Bible and our world.

While Jacob's early life had some strange drama, he ended up becoming a significant character in the history of the world. He made some big mistakes in his life, but he also did some special things that caused him to find favor with God. In his later years, he reconciled with his brother Esau, and he interacted with God in a special encounter. God also changed his name to Israel, so Jacob is actually the father of the Jews and the nation of Israel. Jacob had a complex life and ended up marrying many women and having twelve sons by them. This is obviously going to produce some major problems in the home, and it surely did in this case as well. Jacob, like his parents, played favorites, having a favorite wife and favoring her two sons, Joseph and Benjamin. The other ten brothers were older and resented these two brothers. It seems that while Benjamin was perhaps still a young child, the other ten brothers plotted to kill Joseph when he was just a teenager. However, instead of killing him, they sold Joseph to an Egyptian slave trader and deceived their father into believing that Joseph had been killed by an animal.

Joseph

Joseph could have been filled with hatred, bitterness, and resentment after his brothers had done such a horrible thing to him, however, Joseph loved God, trusted Him, and was obedient to God in spite of the terrible circumstances that Joseph had been dealt. In fact, the Bible indicates that Joseph was one of God's favorite people of all time, and Joseph developed a strong friendship with God. Even though he was a slave, he was willing to work hard and be loyal to his master, so God gave him wisdom and understanding. Joseph's master was a very wealthy man, and he eventually put Joseph in charge of everything he owned. His master's wife, however, was attracted to Joseph and tried numerous times to seduce him. Joseph resisted continually until one day she claimed that he had tried to rape her, and he was then thrown into jail.

While in jail, God still helped Joseph in many ways, and God gave him the ability to interpret dreams. Over time, opportunities came about for him to interpret the dreams of high-ranking individuals, eventually including even the leader of Egypt, Pharaoh. When Joseph told Pharaoh that his dream meant a time of feast followed by great famine was about to occur, Joseph was put in charge of all of Egypt—second only to Pharaoh. As years went by and the famine occurred, Joseph's family heard that Egypt had stockpiled food. Therefore, Jacob sent ten of his sons, Joseph's brothers, there to purchase food.

When Joseph realized that this group of men were his brothers, God gave Joseph incredible wisdom such that Joseph came up with an amazingly clever strategy to reconcile his family back together. It's likely that Joseph now looked like an Egyptian, where it was customary to have all body hair shaved. Since he had also grown from a teenage boy over these past two decades or so, his brothers didn't recognize him. His wise strategy was to keep one of the brothers, have the others go back to their home, and return back to Egypt with Jacob's remaining favorite son, Benjamin. Joseph knew this would be difficult for his father Jacob to allow, since Benjamin was even more special to him since he thought Jacob had died. The brothers had to put their own lives on the line to convince their father to let them take Benjamin to Egypt. Once they returned with Benjamin, Joseph came up with additional wise strategies that led his brothers to admit the horrible thing they had done to their brother Joseph. Once Joseph sensed their remorse, he let them know who he was, he forgave them for what they did to him, and all of Jacob's family moved to Egypt.

So what was the point of Jacob/Israel and his family moving to Egypt? Why did I include this story? Actually, the move to Egypt by the family of Jacob/Israel is one of the most important events in all of human history. If you'll recall earlier, I had mentioned that God had told Jacob's grandfather, Abraham, that he would be the father of a great nation—the most important nation on the globe. How could they be a nation if they were just a small hodge-podge dysfunctional family? When the family of Jacob/Israel moved to Egypt, they were about seventy people total, including Jacob's children, grandchildren, and perhaps great-grandchildren.

If they had not moved to Egypt, they would have continued to intermarry with all the people from the land of the grandfather Abraham and would have never become a special nation family. However, because Egyptians looked down on the Israelites, the Israelites were forced to have the lowly role of shepherds and were kept isolated from the Egyptians and other peoples. This allowed the Israelites to grow by intermarriage within this group of about seventy people. After 400 years, this group grew to a nation-within-a-nation of about 1 million people. They also became a very distinct and cohesive group.

Once this family had become a nation, God was ready to move them to their own land. To facilitate this, an evil Pharaoh arose who began to enslave the Israelites. This Pharaoh also took measures to slow the Israelite's rapid reproduction. He gave orders to have Israelite babies put to death. Luckily, God allowed a baby named Moses—a biblical character you may have heard of, to be born—to be rescued by Pharaoh's own daughter and raised in Pharaoh's palace by an Israelite servant woman—who also happened to be Moses' real mother. The Egyptians did not know that Moses was actually an Israelite until Moses was a grown man.

It's interesting to note that, while Joseph was not a perfect man, he certainly handled adversity with a more faithful attitude than almost anyone else in the Bible. Joseph also had a strong influence in getting his family back to focusing on God, so when 400 years went by with very little detail about the specifics of this time period being covered by the Bible, Moses was taught by his mother about the God of his grandfathers—Abraham, Isaac, and Jacob.

Moses

Moses' life, was not a simple one. As we continue to mention, the devil continued to have an interest in the offspring of Abraham because God had promised that one day Abraham's offspring would lead to the devil's destruction. This no doubt played a role in causing the devil to try to destroy this family. Nonetheless, Moses grew up in the king's palace with everyone thinking he was an Egyptian. His real mother, however, educated Moses about who he was and about the God of Israel. As Moses grew up, he saw the mistreatment of the people of Israel, and later, he actually killed an Egyptian who was abusing an Israelite. Afterwards, he fled from Egypt and spent forty years living in the desert. While in the desert, he met up with some of Abraham's distant relatives and was married. He again became concerned about the Israelites, so God chose to use him as the messenger to deliver the people of Israel from Egypt.

If you have ever watched the epic movie from the 1960's, *The Ten Commandments*, you are familiar with the story of Moses. Some of the most amazing miracles that the world ever witnessed took place during the process of Moses getting Pharaoh to release the Israelites. Pharaoh, and his people, had to suffer many hardships and plagues, including the loss of his first-born son, before Pharaoh finally realized the God of the Israelites was real. He released the Israelites to go free, but then he changed his mind and went after them. The Egyptian army with their chariots and soldiers came in sight of the million Israelites just as they had come to the edge of the Red Sea. God, however, miraculously divided the waters of the Red Sea and allowed the people of Israel to pass through. Once the Israelites were all safely to the other side, God allowed the waters to come crashing back, drowning the Egyptian army in the middle of the Red Sea. This amazing story of the Jews being saved from the Egyptians is even documented in the first few pages of the Muslim's holy book, the Qur'an, which is generally spelled Koran in English translations.

After witnessing such amazing events as this, one might expect that all of the people of Israel and Egypt and those in the surrounding countryside would believe in God and seek His friendship. Surprisingly, however, this awesome display only frightened most of them. As this new nation of Israel now started to journey through the desert, the Spirit of God went with them and protected them in an amazing way. During the day, the Spirit formed a gigantic cloud that protected the people from the heat of the sun.

Each night, the cloud glowed, providing light, protection, and warmth from the typically cold air of the arid desert. God also sent a substance called manna to the ground every morning so that the people would have food to eat, and he brought forth springs of water from the rocks. Despite those who say they would believe in God if He just provided a miracle, the fact is that many of the Israelites who experienced such miracles each day and night still didn't believe in or respect God.

It was during this time in the desert that God gave Moses the Ten Commandments. It was also during this time that God promised to give the people a great land and to help them become a great nation if they would live lives of love for and faith in God. Most of the people never became people of faith, so they all wandered in the wilderness for about forty years before finally doing what God intended for them to do. Part of the reason they were kept in the desert for forty years was to raise a generation of Israelites who would be unwilling to go back to Egypt as slaves. God knew that if He immediately began giving the land to them via warfare and such, many would consider returning to slavery in Egypt instead. This time period helped prepare them, and by allowing many of them to die off, God could help them take control of the land we now know as Israel. Even Moses never actually lived in the new land.

Summary

It's important in reflecting back on the life of Moses—where he fled Egypt and the luxury of palace life at forty years old—to realize that God gave him a forty-year period of life where he had to live in the desert. This forty-year quiet period for Moses was essential for him to be able to later help his people survive and navigate the harsh existence of desert life. This also reminds us that quiet periods of struggle and difficulty in our lives also may be an important step for God to prepare us for important missions and responsibilities that He will someday need us to take on.

Chapter 8

States of the Heart

*B*efore we continue with discussing the Bible and the nation of Israel, it's important to pause and look at what I call the five basic spiritual states that an adult individual can live in. Please keep in mind that these states aren't specifically documented in the Bible. Instead, these are my unique way of trying to help us understand various states of spirituality. I am not intending to box people into certain categories, but rather, I'm trying to provide a way of explaining spirituality that you may find helpful. Please also keep in mind that many of us live our lives with a blend of several of these spiritual states and that we sometimes transition to different states as part of maturing or in response to events that have a high impact on our lives.

- **State 1: Lost** is the natural state where people understand very little if anything about God or spirituality. These people have very little ability to do more than meet their own needs and self-indulgent desires, and they have a limited capacity for love and compassion for others in general. This doesn't mean that they are criminals or thugs necessarily—although some are—but rather that they have a deep emptiness and often long for real love and meaning in their lives. Often, this is the state of younger people who don't want to think about their mortality and who want to enjoy the pleasures this world has to offer.

I've heard people say that there is a hole in each of us that is meant to be filled with God's love and spirit. If we don't fill that hole with God, we will try various forms of the world's pleasures for fulfillment—most of which leads to more emptiness and heartache.

- **State 2: Self-defined morality** is where people recognize the need for some form of morality and these people generally believe that they are good enough to make it into whatever afterlife there is. As we've discussed earlier, defining our own morality doesn't get us into heaven. In America today, we are a divided nation with many people defining their own morality and feeling justified in hating other groups of people because they feel that their version of morality is superior to that of their rivals. Often, this is a state that many people eventually grow in to.

These persons often are members or even leaders of a religious or secular organization who give some portion of their time, skills, and resources to help their religion or certain charity groups. Many of these people hope that, by following certain rules or rituals, they will be accepted into heaven or some peaceful afterlife existence once they die. These people generally love only those who love them, and their basic priority is on meeting their core wants and desires and the needs of their family. These people really don't know God in a personal way and have a significant emptiness inside themselves.

- **State 3: Basic faith** is a state where a person's eyes open and they recognize the colorful beauty and order of this world and that there must be a creator who cares about us. They also may begin to feel this way due to the culture they've grown up in and the values conveyed to them throughout their life. People who have basic faith also pay attention to moral issues, and they want to please their creator. As a result of their respect for the creator, they are also willing to do things that may not make sense to other people, such as praying and helping people in need, and not doing things to harm themselves or others, such as getting drunk, sleeping around, or cheating people. They believe God cares about them and will help them when they have needs or difficult times.

People with basic faith have the ability to help others, believing that God will take care of those who help take care of others, but these people rarely dedicate their lives to helping others establish relationships with God. As a result, people in State 3 can be quite insecure about their salvation and have a very limited relationship with God.

- **State 4: God's Holy Spirit indwelling** inside a person is a state where people understand who Jesus is, who ask God for forgiveness, and invite God's Spirit to become be a part of them (almost all references to people in this state occur after Jesus' death and resurrection in the New Testament). These people begin to know God personally as their lives continue, and although they are not perfect, they have a whole new understanding about life and generally become concerned with the spiritual well-being of everyone.

People who have God's Holy Spirit dwelling within them have the ability to love the unlovable—although they struggle with this through much of their lives. They have surrendered their lives to God and trust that God will meet their needs and will help them meet the needs of others. They often are misunderstood by people who live in States 1, 2, and 3. This is in part because the devil and the demons now see these people as threats to their hope for stopping Christ from someday banishing them to eternal punishment. As a result, the devil and demons work hard to undermine these people in State 4 in the eyes of the rest of the world.

While State 4 people can fall back into living like State 1, 2, or 3 people, I believe that God will never let go of someone who truly repented and invited his Holy Spirit into their heart. Again, the important test for true repentance is when you reach the place where you no longer hate anyone. As I'll discuss as we go forward, even State 4 believers continue to struggle with hate and forgiveness and at times can get angry and lose their faith. However, just us our children may go through seasons of life where they aren't close to their parents, it doesn't mean that their parents will quit loving and caring for them.

People in State 4 are generally much happier people because they truly know God, they know that He watches over them, and they are certain that they'll spend eternity in heaven with God. State 3 people, having basic faith, will also end up in heaven, however, they miss most of the friendship and security that State 4 people have and are more prone to depression and other issues. They also don't have God's Holy Spirit inside them, so they're much less likely to share God's love with others.

From my perspective, State 3 is like hoping to be in love someday and State 4 is actually experiencing the true joy of being in love. I personally believe that many people who come to State 4 during their life struggle at times to stay in State 4. The challenges of life often knock them temporarily out of State 4, and the process of growing in faith and understanding takes many people through seasons of uncertainty.

Either way, the Bible is clear that anyone who ever gave their heart to God though State 3 or 4 will be saved by God and spend eternity in heaven.

- **State 5: Eternal and sinless** is the state of people in heaven who no longer have the ability to sin. Jesus is God the Son and has been with God the Father in heaven since the beginning of time. Although Jesus was tempted to sin during His time on earth, He basically existed in this state during His life on earth. He truly had the proper understanding of how life was meant to be lived.

He lived a perfect loving and godly life on this earth and was able to enjoy life more than anyone ever had because He knew the greatest joy comes from helping people establish relationships with God. However, keep in mind that sometimes we cry when we are experiencing our happiest moments and we can cry when we experience pain and sadness. Jesus wept at times and I believe that he smiled and chuckled quite a bit as well. In conclusion, realize

ETERNITY

that when State 3 or State 4 people die, they also will become State 5 people immediately.

My brief story

At about seventeen years old, in 1981, I was in my freshman year of college and was very much in State 1, trying to satisfy my personal desires. However, I was also frustrated and confused with no real purpose for my life. When I finally recognized this was no way to live, I started attending the Baptist church my mom had taken my brothers and me to during our youth. The pastor who had led the church when I was a child was a nice man, but I don't remember him ever saying anything that really stirred me deep inside. When I was 14, however, the older pastor retired and a new young pastor took the lead. His sermons were very thought provoking and practical, and they began to stir me to think about eternity and what would happen to me when I died. I rarely attended church, however, until my later teen years and then I slowly moved into State 2 and began getting involved with church and trying to be a good person. Nevertheless, I couldn't really change myself. Something still caused me to hate so many things, and I still lived with the sinful and immoral behavior that the entertainment industry and my circle of State 1—lost—friends were encouraging and promoting. I still had a major emptiness in my heart and nothing the world offered really gave me true peace.

At about twenty years old, in 1984, my heart was being stirred and I happened to be walking across my college campus one day—a huge campus with almost 30,000 students—when I bumped into a friend I knew from high school. She also had a ten-minute walk across campus to the building next to the one I was headed to. As we walked and tried to quickly catch up on things, we crossed paths with two nice older gentlemen who were handing out New Testament Bibles. I may have passed up their offer if I had been by myself, but she grabbed two Bibles and gave one to me. A few weeks later—when life had become very difficult—I opened that little white Bible in the privacy of my bedroom, and my life was transformed by the time I had read the first ten chapters of that book. I know that God changed me that night, and I became a State 3 person—a much different person—from that moment on.

I suddenly became aware that many aspects of my life and lifestyle were hurtful to God. Until then, I was a pretty good guy by the world's standards, but deep down I was full of bitterness and hatred and I complained often about people and things that I didn't like. My eyes, however, were opened that evening when I realized that I was complaining about people who God cared greatly about.

We live in a world where so many people have hatred towards others—especially people they really don't know personally. In America and most other places around the world, it's very easy to dislike a person who is running for a political office when they represent your rival party. It also can be easy to speak out against people with negative propaganda that we have never validated. However, it is difficult when such rivalry becomes more personal.

- What if it turns out that a person from the rival party is a close friend to one of your family members and/or best friends?
- What if you find out that this person also played an important role in helping you and your family when you were younger and that your family really loves this person?
- What if you had the chance to meet this person and found them to be very loving and kind?
- Would it change the way you think or speak of them in the future?
- I'm betting that it would.

Similarly, when I realized that much of my anger was directed at a God who I didn't understand and that God loved me and others so very much, I suddenly knew that many of my behaviors were hurtful and disrespectful to God. From that day onward, I discontinued my use of course language and really felt uncomfortable watching movies and TV shows that were violent or contained inappropriate sexual content.

ETERNITY

I'm confident that God went out of His way to have that girl cross paths with me that day because she and I never bumped into each other like that again on any other occasion. Also, I cannot recall any other day when anyone ever passed out Bibles on our campus. Likewise, I am confident that God goes to great lengths to reach the hearts of each of us, but it's truly our decision of whether we open our hearts to Him.

Although I changed that night, I still struggled for the next two years to deal with my new faith and lifestyle among my friends and family. I graduated from college in late 1985 just as I was turning 22, and I was fortunate to have an engineering job waiting for me. Once I settled into work and was planning for marriage, I realized that I had no true Christian friends and that I was really struggling to grow as a Christian. I read the Bible every day, but I felt ineffective at being who God wanted me to be because I had no really close friends who were State 3 or 4 believers. I began praying for months that I would meet people at church or work and really connect with other serious believers.

As the months went on, I began feeling quite frustrated, so one night I begged God to help me make real friendships with other true Christians by having someone I knew and trusted invite me to a Bible Study. The very next day, two friends I worked with were invited to a lunchtime Bible study and asked me to join them. This was the first time in my life I had ever been invited to such an event. I didn't even bother to grab lunch that day but went straight to the study. It turned out that several other young guys I worked with and who I was already beginning to become friends with were the ones leading the Bible study! Within a few months after that, my wife and I started going to church with the guys who led this Bible study. I then learned that it was important for me to invite God's Holy Spirit into my heart. Upon doing so, I became a State 4 person and began caring enough to reach out to my family, friends, co-workers, and neighbors to let them know the truth about God, the Bible, and Christianity.

While the story I just shared correlates my personal life to the five states that I've referred to, the journey is different for everyone. Before I leave these spiritual states, I think it's critical to discuss why these states really matter. I have experienced life in four of these spiritual states, and although I have had some of the most enjoyable moments of my life while living in each of these states, I only felt true peace and contentment in State 4. Much of the world around us lives in State 1 or State 2. In those states, life is about having a good time for yourself. While many of these people can laugh and smile and seem that they are genuinely doing well, the reality is that there is great distress lurking under the façade. Many others in States 1 and 2 show their anger and bitterness in how they carry themselves in most aspects of their behavior, and they're often unwilling to help anyone or trust anyone.

I have also lived in State 3 and have found that to be a difficult existence as well. When living in State 3, I wanted to please God, but I also wanted to be accepted by the world. So, I was torn between hoping that God would save me at life's end and living in obedience to Him. I also found I didn't have any real compassion or concern for anyone besides myself. If I attended church, it was just to make myself feel better and to look good on the outside. Deep down my heart wasn't right. When I lived in States 1, 2 or 3, I found it very difficult to just be alone quietly by myself. I needed to have a significant female in my life, and I had to have the TV on or be on the go every waking minute in an attempt to escape from the reality of my emptiness. I also loved to complain about people and situations that were making my life difficult. It was nearly impossible for me to face the reality that many of my problems were caused by my own selfish desires.

While living in State 4, I find I truly enjoy quiet times alone with God. I wake up each day excited that God is there waiting to talk to me and visit with me as if I am His best friend. Even when difficult situations happen, such as health issues, an unexpected car repair, or friends or family members having major issues, I find that I can relax—most of the time—and let God lead me on the journey. So often, when I stay relaxed, amazing things happen, such as meeting new friends or crossing paths with people who God has sent to help me or who I can help.

Several times when I have gone through aggravating situations that disrupted my scheduled plans, I have bumped into people who gave me leads about business opportunities or who I could help in various ways. When we live in State 4, however, there is still the ongoing challenge of forgiving those who have hurt us or others we care about. However, I have found that it is nearly impossible to even attempt to forgive people when I'm not living in State 4 and letting God's Holy Spirit lead me.

The biggest problem today for those who have been reconciled to God is that we want to live in State 1, 2, or 3 where other people's relationship to God is not much of a concern to us. This was also the problem with most of the Old Testament people who knew God. Although Abraham and Moses knew God, it seems they did not put much effort into sharing God's love with the strangers and neighbors around them. It wasn't until after Jesus' death and resurrection that the Holy Spirit came into the lives of believers and gave people a new kind of love and compassion that world had never seen before.

Summary

In closing, I think it is important to emphasize that while life in State 4 is the best way to live life and to have true peace and joy, life with the Holy Spirit can be quite difficult. God wants us to continually grow to be like His Son, Jesus Christ. When we become a State 4 person, we generally still have our tendencies to be prideful and selfish, and it takes great effort for us to keep our hearts pure. God therefore tests us at times to allow us to grow in our love and faith for Him. There is an old expression, "When God is all you have, you realize God is all you need." For me, I have had struggles where I've lost a job, lost money, or even lost my wife or girlfriend, so I was angry with God for a season. On the other end of the spectrum, when I have had times where things are going very well, I have found that it can be easy to forget about God and not appreciate that He is the one who provided the success and prosperity. Regardless, when we give our hearts to God, He will find a way to sustain us—even when it seems that He may have forgotten us.

Likewise, when we live in State 3 or 4, the devil and the demons want to make our lives difficult, and they often incite other people to hate us or speak negatively about us. For those in State 3 or 4, we may find that we aren't invited to as many social gatherings by our non-Christian friends, and we may even find that friends, family, and our work environment become hostile to us. But it's important to step back and realize that if you ever lived in State 1 or even State 2, you were probably a bit hostile, even gossiped about, or made fun of people who were trying to live godly lives.

Therefore, it's important to love those people and pray for them, because you may be the only person who can influence them to give their hearts to God. For those of us in State 3 or 4, it is extremely likely that someone cared about and prayed for us. Finally, life in State 4 is like winning the lottery—only much better. Similarly to someone who has won the lottery, don't be surprised when many of those around you become jealous and resentful of you when they see your new life in the Lord.

To recap, here are these five states again:
- **State 1: Lost**
- **State 2: Self-Defined Morality**
- **State 3: Basic Faith)**
- **State 4: Dwelling with God's Holy Spirit**
- **State 5: Eternal and Sinless**

Chapter 9

The Bible: The Nation of Israel

We ended Chapter 7 with the family of Israel forming the nation of Israel in the area we refer to as Israel and Palestine of modern day. The process of Israel becoming a nation was an epic journey. The early parts of the Bible are a little fuzzy to determine accurate dates and timelines, although we know within about a thousand years when most of the events occurred. When the Israeli people left Egypt, the timeline we use gets more precise, and many believe the exodus occurred around 1400 BC.

So, what happened during the following 1,400 years before Jesus was born? What has happened since Jesus was born? Before we go into another history lesson, let us look at this nation called Israel and what its purpose really was. When the Israeli people left Egypt, there was no such thing as a Bible for people to base their understanding on. Moses started putting together the Bible after they left Egypt. He was the author of Genesis, although he must have had direct information from God because this is the book we spent so much time discussing earlier. Genesis covers the formation of the world, the beginnings of civilization, and so on. No single person could dream up the events in Genesis and come remotely close to explaining the origin of our world as well as this book does.

This point in the story where the Israeli people leave Egypt is a great time to explain some critical points about God's communication methods with mankind. During the exodus from Egypt, God was physically, visually, and sometimes verbally present before the people. As they traveled through the desert during the day, God was present in a great cloud that led the way. During the night, the cloud was a pillar of fire to light the way for nighttime travel and/or to provide safety and comfort. God continually spoke to Moses verbally. In fact, Moses' first encounter with God was before the exodus when

Moses noticed a burning bush that was somehow not consumed by the fire that engulfed it. He also discovered that the angel of the Lord was present in the same bush. Many believe this angel of the Lord was actually Jesus in his pre-incarnate form, which is similar to encounters that Abraham and Jacob had. This scene is certainly more intimidating than the other encounters where the Lord's appearance was more of a social visit. Not surprisingly, Moses was terrified at first by this encounter and probably wished for another means of interaction that would be less threatening.

We are starting to get to the heart of the matter of God's communication and interaction plans, so pay close attention because misunderstanding about this matter is one of the biggest hang-ups that keeps people from believing in and reconciling themselves to God. It may be helpful to put yourself in the position of god of the universe, so you can understand His situation as it relates to creation.

Let us create plants, animals, and special beings that we can love and enjoy friendships with and give them everything we can to provide for them.

These special beings, however, are complex creatures with spiritual and physical desires such as hunger, love, and so on. They are more than creatures of instinct because they can make moral choices, including whether or not to love their creator, their family, etc. They live in a dimension of time, space, and reality that is unlike the creator's environment of the timeless, spiritual reality. This presents a dilemma of sorts in that this god cannot truly exist in their world and be physically able to have the friendship and personal interaction with everyone that he desires. When this god does try to interact with these special beings, they are afraid of his awesomeness and holiness. This god needs some mechanism by which to interact across this spiritual-verses-physical chasm.

In this modern era, we communicate using smart phones, email, social media, and so on. We should be able to appreciate and comprehend God's dilemma because we cannot physically communicate and interact with everyone we want to without conveying messages through some means of media. The media of 3,400 years ago took form in people passing written and verbal information. These forms are still the most timeless methods we have today. If you wanted to leave instructions for future generations, would you leave a CD, a video tape, a USB device, smoke signals, trained individuals / story tellers, or written instructions? Obviously, the last two choices are the more practical media sources, because they continue to pass through time as standard communication elements.

Similarly, God chose to employ media sources as His interaction with the world. The nation of Israel was to be the instrument to put God's book together. This book was to be more than a manual or rulebook, because it was to be a living story--a book that comes to life and that is active in the lives of people who obey it. God himself calls the Bible the Word of God, and when He came to earth in the form of the person called Jesus, He referred to Himself also as this. While key people from the nation of Israel did a phenomenal job of developing, copying, and protecting God's book, it did a pretty lousy job of living by it and sharing it.

If the nation of Israel had been able to do an effective job of living out and sharing the Bible, God probably could have avoided becoming a part of mankind Himself. However, God knew that the people of Israel had difficulty fulfilling their duty. As we stated a few chapters ago, people want to live their lives in States 1, 2, or 3 with no involvement from God or any concern for others to have involvement with God. It took special circumstances for people to temporarily live in State 4–those truly concerned about how much God loves others. These special circumstances occurred when God's Spirit would come into a person's heart and soul.

The phenomenon of why people do not live up to God's desires is probably the most incredible mystery of human existence. People have an inherent tendency to let physical concerns take priority over almost all other considerations. As some commentaries in recent times have acknowledged, many of us are more concerned about the condition of our bank account than with any other matter. Overemphasis on this one dimension of life causes people to tend to drop down a state or two during their life. The biggest problem in the Christian church today is that the people that God has determined should be in State 4 want to live life in a lower state. Go to most Christian bookstores, and you will find very little material sold that can be distributed to people who have no relationship with God. Most books are about helping us get through this life—State 3. Likewise, a nation full of people at State 3 or lower continues to regress until it either destroys itself or finally wakes up and starts living like State 4 people. Here in America we are paying the price of Christian churches being in a low state for too long.

God wanted the nation of Israel to be a nation different from any other nation or culture before. At that time, the world was full of immorality, slavery, child sacrifices, and idol worship—every kind of wickedness imaginable. We should be able to relate well to this. Although our culture today has been blessed beyond the dreams of every generation before us, most find themselves less happy than ever before. We abort our babies, view immorality all over the media and in the entertainment industry, and find human trafficking and slavery running rampant across the globe. In the few nations that are holding on to some form of moral or religious values, many people are involved in terrorist activities and are willing to kill or torture anyone who doesn't have the same religious views.

God wanted Israel to be a nation of holy, loving people that would love Him, love each other, and obey and teach His commandments. He wanted them to set aside one day each week just to rest and celebrate. This would require them to trust in God because many of the people of Israel worried that they couldn't compete with all of the other cultures if they cut back their labor by more than 15% each week. Nonetheless, after more than forty years of wandering in the wilderness, the people eventually received the land that God had promised to Abraham.

Israel's position over the next 1,400 years and through today has been floundering between States 1 and 2. When the majority of the nation, especially the leadership, lived in State 3, the nation had an easy time winning wars and generally experienced peace and prosperity. When the nation regressed to State 1 or 2, the nation had all sorts of problems and at times was invaded and nearly annihilated by other nations. This nation of Israel has probably been the target of eradication more so than all other peoples and nations combined.

To my knowledge, no one is saying that Argentina, France, or some other country doesn't have a right to exist. However, many nations, primarily the Arab nations discussed earlier, want Israel wiped from the face of the earth. The underlying reason for this again is that the spiritual powers behind the scene—the devil and the demons—continue to try to mess up God's plans for reconciling the world. When the devil sees God make promises that certain events will happen to advance His plans, the devil focuses on preventing them. One would expect the evil beings would eventually give up and go do their own thing or try to reconcile with God, but instead they continue to cause as many problems for God and for us as they can. I do not know why it has to be this way, but the good news is that ultimately the evil side cannot win over any of us if we have established our friendship with God.

The Bible: The Nation Of Israel

For those familiar with the Old Testament and the history of Israel, you probably remember other incredible details about Israel, including the great kings (David, Josiah, etc.), the bad kings (Saul, Manasseh, etc.), the faithful things (David fighting the evil and god-less giant Goliath), the sinful things (David and his adultery and murder), the spectacular things (Jonah swallowed by the fish, followed by his evangelism), and the miraculous things (River Jordan parts for Israel to enter their new land).

This chapter, hopefully, answered some important questions about God's character and plans for this world, and how the nation Israel fits into His plans. In fact, Israel was originally twelve sub nations or tribes, one for each of the sons of Jacob (Israel). Through all the turmoil these sub nations experienced from the days of Moses until the time of Jesus Christ—about 1400 BC to 0 BC, the nation of Israel consolidated over the years into the one nation and at times they did not exist as a nation at all.

Chapter 10

Who Is Jesus?

*I*f you aren't familiar with who Jesus Christ is, consider that of all the billions of people to ever live on this planet, this person Jesus was so significant and controversial that the calendar system that most of the modern world runs on is based on his life. Every scheduled flight that I have ever taken around the world is based on dates relative to the time that Jesus lived on this planet. We are now ready to discuss the most important person to ever live.

As we have followed the history of the world from its creation to its flood and from Abraham to the nation of Israel, God continued to attempt to establish the friendships with mankind that He always desired. He had been involved with some people's lives personally, and He has enabled the nation of Israel to develop His book, which we commonly refer to as the Old Testament of the Bible. The Bible had been written so that everyone can understand who God is and what His purpose is for mankind.

However, something was missing. The people could not seem to understand spiritual matters. The world had become a place of confusion. To shed some insight on how lost and confused the world was, imagine that a disaster occurred that killed everyone over the age of five. The remaining world of babies and preschoolers would be in big trouble. With almost no one able to read or write, no one knowledgeable of how to provide basic necessities, and no one to keep law and order, the chances for these children to survive would be nearly impossible. From a spiritual standpoint, this is how lost and confused most of the world has been and still is to a great deal today. Imagine the impact on this world of orphans if even one caring and knowledgeable adult could come help them and stay with them until they started to mature enough to be able to make it on their own. This is basically what Jesus did.

Let us use another analogy that may also help explain why God came into the world as a person. If you lived in the southern part of the United States and an incredible blizzard occurred during mid-April, many animals that migrate could be caught off-guard by this storm. You might hear noises of birds flying into your front windows as they try to seek relief from the cold and snow. If you had a garage or barn outside that the birds could stay in to survive, could you get the birds to follow you into this safe haven? Of course not! Your intimidating stature would scare them further away. The only way to really help them would be to become a bird and speak to them in their language. This is basically what Jesus did.

Remember when we spoke earlier of how Abraham and Jacob were not intimidated by their encounters with the angel of the Lord? The reason was that He came as a person who they could relate to. In other encounters where He came as God almighty, the people were terrified. This Jesus that we are about to meet is a person that we can all relate to, yet He is also God almighty and the creator of this world.

Many religions have problems with someone saying that Jesus is God. Many claim that He was a good man, a great teacher, a prophet, or even someone not very special at all. None of these are possibilities, since He claims that He was and is God—not just another person. If He was wrong, then He is a liar and a fraud and cannot be classified as anything other than a lunatic. Some religions believe Jesus was just a good guy and good teacher, but that Christians made up the idea that He had claimed to be God.

What evidence would we need to believe that He is God? As we seek to answer this, we can now start to understand why God needed to get the Old Testament of the Bible written before He came into the world. One of the best tools someone can use to prove they have special power or godly ability is to be able to predict events before they occur. Likewise, miraculous signs and wonders performed in person help strengthen the evidence. Jesus employed both of these thoroughly. We have tremendous testimony—in writing—validating many of the events that occurred during Jesus birth, life, death, and resurrection on this earth. We also have tremendous evidence that the predictions of these events were in fact written long before they occurred.

Jesus was born into the world in a way unlike any other person ever born. God intervened in the life of a special young lady who was living as a person of basic faith—my State 3—wherein she had a close relationship with God. She was engaged to be married, but God spoke to her through an angel about His plans for her to be the mother of the God-incarnate child who would forever change the world. She was to become pregnant as a virgin. God also spoke to her husband to be, Joseph, about what was to happen.

These two young people were no doubt under the watchful eye of the evil beings because Jesus' entry into the world was just as traumatic as Moses' had been. When word broke that a baby—one destined to someday become King of Israel—was born in a town near Jerusalem called Bethlehem, those ruling Israel at the time were determined to prevent this. These evil leaders were threatened and issued a mandate to kill all baby boys in the Bethlehem area. Jesus and His parents had to flee to Egypt to escape. Later, when the slaughter had ended, they returned back to Israel and settled in a town quite a distance north of Jerusalem called Nazareth.

It must be more than coincidental that events happened during the lives of several key Biblical characters that nearly took their lives. Joseph was nearly killed by his brothers, but God rescued Joseph from their murderous plot instead placing Joseph into slavery for several years. At the time of Moses' birth, the Pharaoh of Egypt tried to kill all of the Jewish baby boys. At the time of Jesus' birth, King Herod led the region where Jesus was born, and he also tried to kill all of the baby boys. It's clear that the devil was working in the lives and hearts of these rulers in hopes to eliminate key characters who would fulfill God's plan. God, however, never let the devil defeat his ultimate plan.

As Jesus grew up, He was able to remain sinless. This is amazing—even though we do not have a lot of details about His youth. If you have ever raised a child, trying to imagine a child that does not have moments of selfishness, disrespect for parents, or temporary bad attitudes is almost unthinkable. How Jesus completely avoided this as a child, we are not sure. The issue of the age of accountability is not clearly defined by the Bible, so an infant or child behaving childish may not be truly sinful—although it certainly comes from a sinful nature. Regarding the age of accountability, I believe that anyone old enough to significantly worry about their eternal destiny has probably reached that age. Since I am basing my position on taking the Bible literally wherever it seems to warrant this position, let us accept the Bible's position that Jesus was sinless.

In Jesus' time, it's my understanding that a person was not really recognized as an adult until they reached thirty years of age. Therefore, Jesus' life has little written about it until He reached this age. At that point, He spent every aspect of His life fulfilling His mission to change the world. He wanted to show the world how life was intended to be lived. He did not completely avoid taking care of His physical needs in life, but He did put most of His priority to helping others understand the spiritual matters

Who Is Jesus?

of life. He was the most loving and compassionate person to ever live. He healed the sick, He brought dead people back to life, He gave sight to the blind, and He miraculously turned a handful of food into enough to feed thousands of hungry people on several occasions. He also knew when He needed rest and solitude.

Jesus managed to get a lot of the religious leaders of Israel upset. When He explained to them that their responsibility was much more than writing and protecting the Bible, they became hostile toward Him. Jesus did not explain it like I have, but I believe Jesus would support my states of spiritual existence because I think it helps explain a person's spiritual situation. In Jesus' time, the religious leaders were not even in State 3. They thought they were very moral and living in accordance with God's laws, but ultimately, they had no love for God or faith in Him. The leaders found Jesus to be a threat to their religious, political, and economic structure that had made them the elite of their society. Therefore, they decided to put Jesus to death because He was exposing the truth about them to the rest of the nation. They thought killing Him would save their credibility and eliminate the threat of Jesus for good. They forgot that their Bible indicated that if Jesus really was the God-person, He would be killed, but then rise from the dead. The devil also missed this point, because He certainly was in favor of killing Jesus too.

Jesus managed to survive three years in His ministry before He allowed Himself to be killed. During these three years, His life touched countless numbers of people. Many non-Israelites were also touched by His life. He moved many people into a State 3 spiritual existence. Except for a few instances, it was not until after He died that Jesus allowed God's Spirit—the Holy Spirit—to enter the lives of the people whom He knew and become State 4 people. At that point, the lives of those people changed dramatically, and they were finally able to start being the kind of people and friends that God had intended them to be.

We left out a very important person in the life of Jesus. A fellow called John the Baptist played a critical role in Jesus' life and he also validates my position on these spiritual states. The Bible clearly indicates that Jesus must have been a State 5 on my scale, since He was filled with God's Spirit and He was without sin. John the Baptist, however, was the only person before Jesus death to live an entire life in State 4. The Bible indicates that God's Spirit was a part of John even inside his mother's womb. He was also the first person whose entire life was dedicated to restoring people's relationships with God.

There were other important people in Jesus' life, including his twelve followers—disciples as He called them. They were with Jesus during most of His three years of ministering, and they saw all that He did. They could never quite understand who He was or what life was really about until after Jesus died and the Holy Spirit came to be a part of them. None of the twelve ever did much of anything to restore people to God until after His death and resurection occurred. They had only moved into State 3. Once the Spirit came upon them, however, they were not the same people. The disciple Peter had been Jesus' closest friend and ally, but he remained confused about spiritual matters the entire time he was with Jesus. Two minutes after the Holy Spirit came into him, however, he was explaining to thousands of people exactly who Jesus is, what the Bible is all about, and helping restore the people to God.

Anyone who has been reading up to this point is certainly ready to move into spiritual State 4—if you are not already there—and touch the lives of family, friends, neighbors, and the world with the truth just as Peter did. If you need more information then keep reading on. If you are ready to get things right with God, then all you have to do is apologize—repent—for not having loved God. Ask Him to accept you as His child, to acknowledge your love for Him before others, and God will be glad to come and give you the life and friendship with Him that you both long for. If this sounds too simple, we will debate the matter in more detail before we are done. In Matthew, Chapter 10, Verses 32–33, Jesus stated, "Whoever acknowledges me before others, I will also acknowledge him before my Father in heaven. But whoever disowns me before others, I will disown before my Father in heaven."

As we stated earlier, part of being able to prove that Jesus is God is strongly supported by how many written predictions He fulfilled. His life was an on-going fulfillment of the Old Testament predictions about the God-person who was to come into the world. For instance, His birth by a virgin, the place of His birth, his flight to Egypt to escape the slaughter of innocent babies, the time of His death, the method of His death, and numerous other events were clearly described in many Old Testament passages. We can find no predictions that were wrongly fulfilled. There are many other biblical predictions still unfulfilled because the world is not yet in its final eternal state.

People throughout the ages have been affected by the wrongful behavior of others. People have been verbally abused, murdered, tortured, starved, and so on. We all have a part of us that wants to see the people who do these things suffer as well. Many people would not have been upset if Hitler had been tortured, starved, and burned alive if the Allies had been able to capture him. Likewise, there is a judgment and penalty from God for all who do these things.

The bad news is that in God's eyes we are all guilty. God says that if we ever thought of murdering someone, we are as guilty as someone who did. God says that, if we have anyone that we do not truly love and care for, our lack of love is the ultimate guilt. The proper perspective even for Hitler should be sorrow that he could be led to do what he did, yet hope that he got right with God before he died. I want no one to be separated from God, although I still at times am guilty of being wrongly upset with people. If Hitler made amends with God before he died, imagine the impact on the people who end up in heaven from getting an apology from him. It may be the ultimate challenge of forgiveness for those individuals whom he personally wronged, but when the films of each of our lives gets played before God, the forgiveness needed from God for each of us will be even greater than we can imagine because everything wrong we have done has hurt Him.

If we had been put in one of Hitler's death camps and became a Christian while there, and we were given the chance to make a statement to Hitler himself before being killed, what might we say? It would be easy to tell him we hoped he burned in hell for what he had done. Since Hitler was actually very well-versed in the Bible, especially the Old Testament books, he felt he was justified to eliminate the Jews for their failure to believe in Jesus. So, a better thing to tell him would be that his justification for destroying the Jews for lack of belief misses the whole point. The only authority Hitler had in the matter was to explain Jesus to the Jews, not kill them for what they had not been able to understand. Also, knowing that Hitler really had to be confused himself about religion and such to do all this in the first place, it would not hurt to quiz him on his qualifications as a Christian and help him find the right answers. Lastly, telling him that you personally forgive him and God can still forgive him even if he goes ahead with killing you sounds sort of weak, but it is the most critical point to make. It then becomes his conscience that has to struggle with the guilt of killing someone who actually cared about him.

This issue of forgiveness is still tough for almost all of us, especially if we do not know God. If some person pushed your child out a window and killed them, could you ever forgive them? What if the person who pushed was your other child? Hopefully, something like this will never occur in your family, but if it did, then your ability to forgive the surviving child is probably going to be the most critical matter this child will deal with for the rest of his or her life. If you cannot forgive, then this child may never forgive himself or anyone else and has greater likelihood to die unreconciled to God. If you can forgive, then this child will likely be able forgive others in his life and be reconciled to God.

Now, if generally good people have been put through horrible treatment at times, it is no surprise that Jesus also had to suffer such treatment. The description of Jesus' death is one of the worst experiences that any person on the face of the earth has ever endured, especially an innocent man. He was put through an illegal, unjust trial where he had no legal counsel. He was stripped, brutally beaten, and tortured by the Roman military that represented the police and jailers of Israel during Jesus' time. He was crucified, which was one of the most painful means of execution ever invented. In his case, huge spikes were driven through his hands or wrists and feet into a large wooden cross. The cross was then mounted upright, and the victim was left there until death occurred. This could take hours or possibly days.

As we look at why Jesus died, our previous discussion about justice and sacrifice starts to play a key role. First, Jesus' death was the substitution for evil people who deserved to be beaten, tortured, starved, and brutally murdered for having done such things to others. Second, since we concluded that our lack of love for God and for the people of the world who are all cousins to us make us as guilty as any other evil person, then each of us also deserves to endure this. Therefore, Jesus took our place.

There are other aspects about Jesus' death that we need to discuss. We did not mention much about Jewish laws and customs in earlier parts of the book, but the Old Testament is filled with rules and laws about sacrificing money, livestock, and such on regular intervals to serve as payment for sins. No sins can be forgiven in Jewish law without something having to lose its life. This is another reason that Jesus actually had to die.

In addition, several amazing physical events occurred at the moment of His death, which should have convinced everyone of who He really was, but it did not seem to. First, Jesus' death happened to come on the one special day of the year when the nation of Israel makes its most special sacrifices to God for their sins—Passover. This special day commemorates God's exempting Israel from the plagues He was bringing on the people of Egypt during Moses' time when Israel was held captive as slaves to the Egyptians. Second, while He was on the cross, an eclipse-type event occurred, causing darkness for three hours during the middle of the day. Third, at the moment of Jesus death, an earthquake occurred, rocks were split, and many people who had died of faith—State 3 people—came out of their tombs. Most people witnessing this should have believed that Jesus was someone of unearthly power.

Finally, the veil of the temple, which only a high priest of the Jews was allowed to pass beyond, was magically torn in two in front of many people's eyes. This indicated that because of Jesus' death, God had changed the method by which people interface with Him. The high priest was no longer the intermediary between regular people and God. Instead, every individual could now relate directly with God. Whether they understood this at the time seems unlikely. However, this incredible miracle should have increased their belief that Jesus truly was more than a man for it to occur at the moment of His death.

Another tremendous aspect surrounding Jesus' death is that it served as proof that there is life after death. Many people doubt that Jesus actually is alive today, but the Biblical and historical accounts of Jesus being seen alive after He was definitely declared to be dead is very strong. More than 500 people witnessed encounters with the resurrected Jesus over about a forty-day period after his crucifixion. They talked with him and even ate with him. Also, many people witnessed Him actually ascend from earth into the heavens. If it really is true that Jesus survived the grave, and it is, then it gives us all hope for our future.

The greatest aspect of all about what Jesus did for us, however, was to guarantee that those who love Him will spend eternity in heaven. While the famous Psalm 23 of the Old Testament strongly confirms eternal life for people of faith, most people of the Old Testament probably struggled with whether they were truly saved because of the ongoing sacrifices for sin and their inability to keep the laws and the Ten Commandments. Jesus left us with the promise that He would never let anyone who reconciles himself to God be denied eternal life—regardless of what mistakes the person makes the rest of his life. This freedom, when coupled with the ability to directly communicate to Jesus through prayer, is probably the most exciting aspect of Christian life. It is more reassuring than winning a forty-million-dollar lottery because this never ends.

A lot of cults and confused Christians disagree with me on this point of God's assurance of salvation. As a result, they spend their spiritual life continually trying to earn and re-earn their salvation under the constant stress of scoring enough points to appease God. This misses the whole point of faith and trust in God, because the burden then becomes making God trust in you. If things happen that stop you from meeting your spiritual agenda, then it becomes your responsibility to work around it. If you become disabled, you may become frustrated about losing your salvation because you cannot work as hard to please God. Real faith is a relaxed life that knows that God is in charge and that we can only work with the resources and circumstances God provides us. One of the devil's favorite tools for messing up Christians is to get them to believe that they have to earn their salvation. Here again, life after death is guaranteed, but whether we spend it with God in heaven or without God in hell is our choice. Once we choose to be reconciled to God, the issue is settled forever—even if we continue to struggle or have doubts at times.

ETERNITY

Summary

In conclusion, Jesus Christ is God Almighty Himself. He came to live on earth for a brief period to transform us into people finally capable of loving Him and living lives of faith and love for this world.

Chapter 11

What Happens After We Die?

*H*eaven or hell? This cannot be real, can it? I have mentioned this loving God who wants people to love him. How then can the word hell even come from this loving God? Surely there is no eternal hell, right?

I sometimes wish the answer to this was no. I also sometimes wish that people were only punished for some period of time for the wrong they did (like prisons and jails) and then they were released to heaven. Then we could all do our best, enjoy life, and eventually end up in paradise. Our friends and family would all eventually get there too, so we really would not have to worry about anything but enjoying ourselves and our life on this earth, right? If the idea were to pop into our head to take our money, leave our family destitute, and go live an exciting promiscuous life, then what would be the harm? The family would survive, and we would all be pals someday in heaven, right? That sort of thing may work on television or in movies, but with God there is an ultimate justice system, and heaven is for those who truly love God and who find saving grace during their life on earth. It is not exactly what I would have come up with, but at least we all have the ability to choose our final destiny, and for those who choose to love God, the final destiny is far better than deserved. When we all experience eternity, I believe we will all understand God's love and justice, but there are things about good and evil that we will struggle to grasp on this side of eternity.

I believe all people are haunted by the notion of death, life after death, judgment, and so on. I do believe that animals are concerned about staying alive and surviving, but there is no indication that they have any sense of life after death, because God made people with a higher level of complexity. Just as animals are more complex than plants, so too, people have a complex moral soul and spirit that animals do not. Whether our pets will be waiting for us in heaven, however, I do not know. The Bible indicates that there will be animals in the end times and that the lion will lie down with the lamb. Whether these will be new animals or resurrected animals, I also do not know, and I will not venture into that subject in this book. This book is concerned about the fate of human beings based on my love for them and God's love for them—including my daughters, brothers, other family members, friends, neighbors, co-workers, and the friends and families of all these different individuals.

Reconciliation

Have these worries about our death caused us to invent religion as a crutch to mask our concerns? Was religion just invented to help people attempt to control the uncontrollable, such as the weather, economics, and our health? Many like to believe this. That, however, is about all that they are willing to believe. This book and its strong argument lending credibility to the Bible will be laughed at by some.

ETERNITY

When Jesus hung on the cross, an eclipse occurred, and at the moment of His death, an earthquake occurred. While many laughed at Him as they hung Him on the cross, I'm sure the laughter ended as those incredible events happened, but even those incredible miracles weren't enough to change the hearts and beliefs of most of those who observed those incidents. For some, no amount of information is enough to convince them otherwise. I'm sure that those who witnessed Jesus' death all believe now that He is the Son of God, but for those who never gave their heart to God during their lifetime, they are spending eternity in hell and forever regretting their decision not to believe.

For us to cross the hurdles that can separate us from God, it takes intervention beyond our own abilities, yet we are 100% responsible for whether we become believers or not. This is another great mystery, but it is one that we are each responsible for working through. Becoming a Christian is very simple, yet it is also the hardest thing a person can do. It would be a very difficult task for anyone to go on national television and admit wrongdoing in front of everyone they know and those they do not know, but the actual exercise of this is very simple. Likewise, anyone can join a religion, club, or organization where your past does not matter. God is not out to humiliate people who want to know Him, but because He knows every thought we've ever had and every sinful action we've ever done, we cannot be reconciled until we apologize to Him and ask for His forgiveness.

Concerning the grounds for reconciliation, if the only way to restore our friendship with people on earth that we have hurt is admitting our offence and apologizing to the hurt party, which can be very difficult for us to do, it still makes sense that this is the only reconciliation method with God.

Heaven or Hell?

So what are you ready to believe?. What the future holds for those who die unreconciled with God is not a fun picture. There are various forms of afterlife existence. The souls of people who reconciled themselves to God before they died are currently in a semi-spiritual yet physical place called heaven,

Paradise, Abraham's side or Abraham's bosom. The souls of people who died unreconciled to God are currently in another semi-spiritual yet physical place called hell, death or Hades. At the end of time, those reconciled with God will be given new bodies and live again in a new physical world called the new heaven or new Jerusalem. Those unreconciled to God and those already in hell will also be given new bodies at the end of time, but they will then be cast along with the devil and the demons into a permanent form of hell called the lake of fire.

The Book of Luke, Chapter 16, Verses 19–31, describes both of the current afterlife places, heaven and hell. I warn you that reading the following passage may keep you up tonight whether you are a Christian already or not. If you are, you may decide it is time to make a list of your friends that you need to go share this with. If you are not a Christian, I hope you will genuinely investigate these critical matters further.

Luke 16:19–31

19. "There was a rich man who was dressed in purple and fine linen and lived in luxury every day.
20. At his gate was laid a beggar named Lazarus, covered with sores
21. and longing to eat what fell from the rich man's table. Even the dogs came and licked his sores.
22. The time came when the beggar died and the angels carried him to Abraham's side. The rich man also died and was buried.
23. In hell, where he was in torment, he looked up and saw Abraham far away, with Lazarus by his side.
24. So he called to him, 'Father Abraham, have pity on me and send Lazarus to dip the tip of his finger in water and cool my tongue, because I am in agony in this fire.'
25. But Abraham replied, 'Son, remember that in your lifetime you received your good things, while Lazarus received bad things, but now he is comforted here and you are in agony.

26. And besides all this, between us and you a great chasm has been fixed, so that those who want to go from here to you cannot, nor can anyone cross over from there to us.'
27. He answered, 'Then I beg you, father, send Lazarus to my father's house,
28. for I have five brothers. Let him warn them, so that they will not also come to this place of torment.'
29. Abraham replied, 'They have Moses and the Prophets; let them listen to them.'
30. 'No, father Abraham,' he said, 'but if someone from the dead goes to them, they will repent.'
31. He said to him, 'If they do not listen to Moses and the Prophets, they will not be convinced even if someone rises from the dead.'"

This passage, in my opinion, is the most intense scene of horror and shock that I have ever encountered. This person's agony will never end. Shockingly, many people can scoff at the notion of hell or refuse to believe it. However, even if there is the remotest possibility of spending eternity in burning hell, it certainly warrants some investigation. You can call me a hell-and-damnation type of person if you choose, but I am not going to leave this part out because the Bible makes it very clear that hell is real. Hell is not just some analogy of the difficulties of living in this world. I care too much to let those still alive here die without warning them clearly about hell.

This passage has nothing to do with rich verses poor or sick verses healthy. This story relates two individuals whose lives crossed paths, but whose final destinies were completely opposite because only one of the two became reconciled with God during his life on earth. Their lives on earth could not have been more different either. There is nothing special about these specific people other than that their story helps us understand more about life, mercy, materialism, and relationships. The eternal states of heaven and hell apply to everyone who has ever lived and died, and the final outcome of these two people could easily have been reversed. There are no doubt many cases where people in Lazarus' condition never reconcile themselves to God, although they may have had rich and not so rich people reach

ETERNITY

out and try to help them both physically and spiritually during their life.

Nevertheless, here are a few critical aspects of this passage.

[1] People have a conscious existence after death.

[2] People have memory of their life on earth.

[3] Hell is a place of ultimate physical torment.

[4] There is no second chance for repentance after death.

[5] The dead in hell cannot communicate with the living, although a few instances have occurred where the dead in heaven communicated with the living, such as Samuel's appearance to Saul and Moses and Elijah's appearance with Jesus).

[6] There are no atheists in the afterlife.

[7] Those in hell can see and recognize those in heaven and vice versa.

[8] Those in hell cannot cross over the chasm into heaven and vice versa.

I have heard people make statements such as the following:

a. If there is a hell, then I will rule the place.
b. At least I will be with my companions in hell.
c. My hell has been living this life on this earth.
d. If God is evil enough to condemn me to hell for my ignorance, then that is fine with me.

This passage from the Book of Luke definitely did not show the rich man having a good time with his buddies as they ruled this new kingdom, unless the torture chamber and dungeon are considered a highly desirable places to be. Many believe that another aspect of being in hell is complete isolation with the exception of having the ability to see those in heaven. Additionally, life on this earth has never been as bad for anyone as what this scene showed hell to be. If God could speak to Moses through a burning bush that was not consumed by the fire that engulfed it, then He can also engulf the soul of a person in hell in flames of fire forever as well. In fact, the rich man's agony is so great that he would even today appreciate the slightest drop of water for only a second of relief. Finally, those in hell realize it is their own fault for being there, they knew the truth but chose not to repent, and they suddenly want to become State 4 people and save their friends and family from this same fate. Unfortunately, it is too late for them to change their situation or to warn their friends.

Summary

Although I have not put as much emphasis on how great heaven will be compared to how horrible hell will be, I believe that if evil men can outwardly live in beautiful places on this earth and enjoy lavish lifestyles and vacations, heaven will be phenomenally better than the best this earth has to offer. The only negative for those in heaven will be seeing those across the chasm suffering forever in hell, including old friends and family members. The reason I am writing this book is because I hope not to see anyone I have known on earth spending eternity in hell. I also wish that my friends would also share this knowledge and love, so no one they know will end up in hell. The Bible seems to indicate, however, that in the final abode of the reconciled in this New Jerusalem every tear will be wiped away from those in heaven, and people will no longer see or remember those in hell. However, those residing in the lake of fire will be able to see the people they knew enjoying life in this new heaven on earth.

I've had some people ask me how anyone could enjoy being in heaven when they know that people they cared about are burning in hell. I personally believe and have heard other Christian leaders state that in heaven we may still be able to compartmentalize our minds somewhat—just as we do in this life. For instance, true followers of God should be greatly saddened and concerned when we see a TV commercial showing us starving children. Nonetheless, we can find ourselves moments later meeting up with friends and family and smiling, laughing, and enjoying more food and drinks than we could possibly eat. Likewise, I think that we will have moments of sadness in heaven, but we'll also be able to set the sad thoughts aside at times and smile, laugh, and

ETERNITY

enjoy being with the Lord and our family, friends, ancestors, and new friends.

Chapter 12

Who Can Be Saved?

"Who can be saved?" Now. let's answer another very tough question. As I address the very important matter of who can be saved, I want to make it clear—very clear—that I am not passing judgment or condemning any religious group as a whole. There are too many passages in both the Old and New Testament of the Bible that indicate that people throughout the world will spend eternity with God in heaven. In fact, Jesus was more impressed by the faith, love, and understanding of many non-Jews than He was of His own special people. While the Bible is clear that many Jews such as David and Moses are in heaven with God today, it also refers to the Queen of the South being one of those who will judge the world at the end of time. The Queen of the South was the Queen of Sheba—also referred to as modern day Ethiopia—who had enough concern about her relationship with God that she traveled a great distance to hear the godly wisdom of the great king of Israel, David's son, Solomon. It is believed that Ethiopia was still somewhat of a God-fearing nation when Jesus was alive on the earth about a thousand years after Solomon died.

While some Christians strictly believe that only those who specifically respond to the New Testament message about Jesus can acquire salvation, the New Testament book of Hebrews and other passages strongly indicate that people before Jesus' time were saved because they believed and understood that they could be reconciled with God and forgiven of their sins. In addition, Jesus did exist from the start of eternity, because He was and is God. Just as I can be a father to my children, a friend to many, and a son to my parents, God can be multidimensional, as he is capable of being God the Father, God the Son, and God our personal friend all at the same time. There is certainly more complexity to this matter, but we are not entitled in this life to understand every matter clearly. Even as young children cannot comprehend the complex science of physics, their lack of comprehension does not invalidate its affects upon their world.

Remember that God cares about every person on the planet. I've heard it said that God does not have any grandchildren—only children. Therefore, God makes great effort to reach every person born on this planet so that we'll turn our hearts to Him and build the close, loving relationship He desires to have with each of us. The first generations of people on this globe did not have a Bible to guide them. Many people and civilizations have been blocked from knowing about the God of Israel and the story of Jesus Christ coming to earth. So how can God hold all people who have ever lived on earth accountable for their needing to know there is a God and their needing to repent?

The best Bible passage I have found to explain how God can hold each of us accountable comes from the Book of Romans, Chapter 1, Verses 16–32.

16 For I am not ashamed of the gospel, because it is the power of God that brings salvation to everyone who believes: first to the Jew, then to the Gentile.

17 For in the gospel the righteousness of God is revealed—a righteousness that is by faith from first to last, just as it is written: "The righteous will live by faith."

18 The wrath of God is being revealed from heaven against all the godlessness and wickedness of people, who suppress the truth by their wickedness,

19 since what may be known about God is plain to them, because God has made it plain to them.

20 For since the creation of the world God's invisible qualities—his eternal power and divine nature—have been clearly seen, being understood from what has been made, so that people are without excuse.

21 For although they knew God, they neither glorified him as God nor gave thanks to him,

but their thinking became futile and their foolish hearts were darkened.

22 Although they claimed to be wise, they became fools

23 and exchanged the glory of the immortal God for images made to look like a mortal human being and birds and animals and reptiles.

24 Therefore God gave them over in the sinful desires of their hearts to sexual impurity for the degrading of their bodies with one another.

25 They exchanged the truth about God for a lie, and worshiped and served created things rather than the Creator—who is forever praised. Amen.

26 Because of this, God gave them over to shameful lusts. Even their women exchanged natural sexual relations for unnatural ones.

27 In the same way the men also abandoned natural relations with women and were inflamed with lust for one another. Men committed shameful acts with other men, and received in themselves the due penalty for their error.

28 Furthermore, just as they did not think it worthwhile to retain the knowledge of God, so God gave them over to a depraved mind, so that they do what ought not to be done.

29 They have become filled with every kind of wickedness, evil, greed and depravity. They are full of envy, murder, strife, deceit and malice. They are gossips,

30 slanderers, God-haters, insolent, arrogant and boastful; they invent ways of doing evil; they disobey their parents;

31 they have no understanding, no fidelity, no love, no mercy.

32 Although they know God's righteous decree that those who do such things deserve death, they not only continue to do these very things but also approve of those who practice them.

Remember, God made this world in all its beauty—blue skies, green grass, white snow, yellow, pink, and purple flowers, rainbows, and gorgeous colorful sunrises and sunsets. He also created us with the knowledge of right from wrong, and good from evil.

So while many have lived and died without having much of the information I've shared in this book, God has given everyone enough information to know that He is real, that He loves us, that He watches over us, and that He will provide for us so that we don't need to lie, steal, cheat, exploit, or gossip in order for us to survive in this life or the eternity to come. When we finally see the story of our life, each of us—including every person ever born—will see how God watched over us and loved us, even if we lived thousands of years ago on a remote island far from the nation of Israel or before the nation of Israel even existed. We will also see that for much of the evil we had experienced or caused, God was using this or allowing this to help turn our hearts toward Him.

So if God judges each of us individually, why does Christianity matter? Won't a certain percentage of people be saved—regardless of their religious influence? While I believe that some people brought up with non-Christian backgrounds will be saved, the Bible indicates that a much higher percentage of people will be saved where true Christian believers reach out and tell non-Christians about God and His Son Jesus Christ. Also, as stated earlier, only people who understand God's grace through Jesus and who invite the Holy Spirit into their lives will truly experience real godly joy and peace on this side of eternity. Only these State 4 people will be driven by love to share it with their friends, family, neighbors, co-workers, and even people at the remotest parts of the world. Others who have been saved—State 3 people—will always be somewhat troubled deep-down inside themselves as to whether they really are saved.

State 4 people also have periods in their life where they worry that they've hurt God too much. They will also be troubled and will lack true peace. I've gone through a season of falling from State 4, and I can attest to the worry and lack of peace that I had during that time. However, I now understand how God used that time in my journey to help me trust even more in Him. Almost every godly character in the Bible had some season or event where they disobeyed God or turned their back on Him temporarily, so don't condemn yourself if you've given your heart to God but still sin at times and then feel distant from God.

So what are you willing to believe? There's a story of a pastor who was chatting with a dairy farmer. The farmer stated that he wouldn't believe what he didn't fully understand. The pastor then asked him, "Do you understand how a brown cow eats green grass and produce white milk?"

Responsibility to Family or God?

While many people may hope that I conclude that there are many paths that lead to God, I believe that the Bible is clear—there is only one path to God. We must all recognize the true God of heaven, repent to Him, reconcile ourselves with people we've hurt, and live the rest of our lives as loyal friends of God—even though we may struggle at times to love and avoid sinful behavior. Those who have been informed over the past 2,000 years about Jesus Christ were capable of having the Holy Spirit dwell within them and could live with an even closer relationship with God. Being saved and having the basic faith of being in State 3 is like one knows about being in love and hopes to someday experience it. However, being in State 4 and having the Holy Spirit in our hearts is like the incredibly thrilling experience of actually being in love.

I have friends who were raised with a religious upbringing that was not based on Christianity. Many aspects to their religion are based on some basic moral concepts or far-fetched and unproven superstitions and ideas based on the writings of one person. In chatting with several people who have told me they believe in reincarnation, I've asked them if they think there are more people on the earth now than there were 1,000 years ago. They typically say yes, but when I asked what determines whether a person is reincarnated or a newborn person, I see signs that they are finally starting to think deeper about this. As of my writing of this book, no one thus far has presented me any true basis to support the concept of reincarnation.

I also have had some friends who've grown up with other religions tell me that if they become a Christian it would be a slap in the face to their parents, their family, and their ancestors who have believed in this religion. However, if their parents never understood God to the level that this book teaches, then God will judge their family and ancestors on whether they loved God and people with the knowledge of God and good and evil that they were exposed to. If you now know much more about God's interactions with humanity and want to give your heart to Jesus, but you worry about offending your family and their long-held heritage, then consider the story of my dad.

My dad was a good guy, but he struggled with alcohol when he reached his mid-forties. My mom took my brothers and me to church when we were kids, but dad never joined us. When I became a Christian at age 20, I became very concerned about my family and friends. Over a period of about twenty years, I spoke with my dad as respectfully as I could. I once told him that I respected him, but I wanted him to tell me if he thought my being a Christian was wrong and a waste of time. After years of hearing my questions and comments like these along with countless prayers for and encouragement to my dad from other family members and friends, dad finally gave his heart to God at seventy-eight years old.

Summary

In conclusion to "Who Can Be Saved?," any person can be saved if they give their hearts to the true God and creator of this world based on what I've explained. For a person to be right with God, a person has to apologize or repent for not having loved God, must ask God to accept them as His child, change from sinful and evil ways, and be willing to acknowledge their love of God before others.

Chapter 13

Time to Make a Change?

The purpose of this book is to explain the fundamental plan of salvation that many of us have been somewhat exposed to in our life. Many of us have been told something like, "We are sinners, but if we repent and believe in the name of Jesus then we can have eternal life." While this is sufficient to convince some about Christianity, for me and most of the people I speak with, it leaves a lot of questions unanswered. This book is an attempt to address a lot of the questions that many of us need answered. While there are questions you may come up with that I have not—or cannot—answer, I hope enough answers have been provided to at least allow you to consider Christianity for yourself.

Since terms such as sin, repentance, and faith are not commonly used in society today, many people do not really understand these basic concepts as they relate to salvation and God. I hope that I have clarified what sin and repentance are through the examples used in this book. Remember the analogy of someone calling us worthless idiots? We discussed how the only way that person could truly reconcile himself or herself to us would be through admitting that he said something terrible about us and sincerely apologizing to us. Likewise, this is the only way for us to reconcile ourselves to God, who we have hurt through the things we have said and done.

There is one more important term—faith—that we have not discussed much, but I think we now have enough of a foundation to address this misunderstand concept.

Faith

Reconciliation with God is an issue not only of apologizing to God, but it incorporates faith that there is a God, faith that this God is who the Bible says He is, faith that God loves me, faith that God will forgive me if I ask, faith that God will take care of me even in times of financial hardships or other difficulties, and faith that God will let me spend eternity with Him. Although no one likes to talk about giving money, the Bible tells us that a person should try to give at least a tenth of what they make—a tithe—to the church. After all, it is actually a tenth of what God allowed us to make. However, what if you are currently making less than you can survive on? Do you borrow from savings or go into debt to give this tithe? I've had to make exceptions to my normal tithing during periods of unemployment in my life, and I think it's something we each have to pray to God carefully about. The question for each of us is whether we really believe in God and that He is who he says is.

As another example, let us assume that we have an exam and that we study as hard as we can for it. During the test, we struggle to remember the answers to some of the questions, but the teacher leaves, and we have the opportunity to glance at our notes. Do we trust that God will honor us for being honest and doing our best on the test, or do we rationalize that we really need to score well on this test and glance at our notes? Notice how rationale seems to go against faith and honesty? The truth is that people who cheat their way through school and through life eventually earn their way into responsibilities they find they cannot handle. People who try as hard as they can but remain faithful and honest may not make the highest scores, but chances are that the responsibilities they will be given throughout life will match their abilities.

When our computer or car breaks down, causing us to get home late from work and miss the television show we wanted to watch, how do we usually respond? Some of us will probably become upset enough that others will not want to be around us. A person of faith, however, finds it easier to relax through this situation, realizing that an opportunity may come such as seeing an old friend or meeting someone new they can befriend a result of getting their car or computer repaired.

A few years ago, I had my own business. However, the business was struggling, and I was considering the idea of selling it to another company. Just as I was preparing all the documentation for the sale, there were suddenly incredible news reports about the abortion industry that I knew God wanted me to speak out about. Up until that point, I had kept my political and social views away from social media. However, as I sensed God wanted me to take action, I remember praying and saying, "Lord, this could impact my ability to sell the company if the buying company doesn't like my position on this matter." I then sensed God was asking me, "Do you really want to join a company who won't allow you to speak out about what's right?" I realized God was right, and I said, "Lord I'll obey you and let you deal with the consequences."

I made some posts on Facebook about the truth—and evils—of the abortion industry, and suddenly the deal to sell my company quickly began to unravel. Somehow though, I felt a special peace and knew that God would find a way to take care of me, as He had done my whole life. Over the next few weeks, my business boomed like it never had before and it had its most profitable periods of all time. Now, God didn't have to bless my business, and God owed me nothing. Nevertheless, as He's done on countless occasions throughout my life, he allowed my faithfulness to produce great blessings beyond my control and exceeding my expectations.

Few people respond to situations this way, and I have failed to respond with faith myself on so many occasions, but this was how Jesus reacted when problems occurred or when plans got changed. A person of faith should generally be a relaxed, stable person who can stay in control of their emotions and thoughts. In reality, none of us are able to keep our composure at all times and in all situations. The Christian, however, should find the ability to respond in faith much more often than before he was a Christian. When we lose our composure, it is easy for us to say or do something we will regret. Likewise, losing our composure really means lacking faith to believe God is ready to help us through a difficult situation, confirming what the book of Romans, Chapter 14, Verse 23 states "... and everything that does not come from faith is sin..."

Time To Make A Change?

Gaining Perspective

Let us assume our daughter has brought home her new boyfriend and he appears to be a completely opposite type of person we had in mind for her to date. Do we respond like Archie Bunker from the 1970s television show *All in the Family* and call her boyfriend a meathead? Do we risk destroying the relationship we have with our daughter? Alternatively, do we assume that if our daughter thinks this person is special then there must be something good about him? After all, if we raised our daughter correctly, she should have good judgment, right? A better response than telling our daughter that she made a bad choice would be to ask our daughter what attracted her to this person and listen to what she says. Chances are, if she did use bad judgment, she will probably start to recognize this herself when she analyzes her thoughts and emotions. If she used good judgment, then you will probably find reasons to feel good about this person from hearing her perspective.

It is interesting that most of the sinful things we do are not that bad from a rational standpoint. It certainly seems irrational to believe in some God we cannot see, to stay married to a person we do not always get along with, to not get upset when things go wrong, or to donate money that we could use for other things. It also seemed irrational for Adam and Eve to be restricted from eating from a certain tree. Maybe this is why some people like to refer to the word rationalize as rational lies. This conflict between faith and rationalization is related to the wants, desires, and addictions that we develop in our lives.

Impediments to Faith

As we start to face the ultimate question of who God is to us—whether there is no God, whether He is only an onlooker, whether He is an unstable and unpredictable force who we need to impress in order to get eternal life, or whether He is a God of love and judgment as the Bible says He is—we need to look at what stands between us and God.

For most people, coming to terms with God seems about as much fun as going on trial, where every bad or embarrassing thing we have ever done will be brought out for everyone to ridicule and laugh at. It is no wonder that we get uncomfortable bringing up the subject of God, Jesus, heaven, and hell. Earlier, we discussed that many people fear having to give up things in order to get right with God. Most have a problem with pride and rivalry, feeling that they could not handle the ridicule and loss of respect they might get from friends and family if they join the other side and start talking about God, attending church, reading their Bible, or refusing to participate in wrongful behavior. They may also feel that they could not stop certain behaviors, and therefore God would have no use for them. They may also feel that if God could not forgive the things they have done then neither could the people they have hurt. Many also fear that the people or church inviting them to be reconciled to God are just another group of religious fanatics who will cause them unnecessary turmoil and humiliation.

ETERNITY

No matter how we approach things, getting involved in anything new, whether it be a new job, new school, new social group, or new church, will be a somewhat uncomfortable experience. If you decide to reconcile yourself to God, then expect some changes to occur in your life and expect some periods of major discomfort at first. If you won a mega-lottery or massive inheritance that you would receive proceeds from starting in ten years, wouldn't you be excited? Salvation with God is far better than all the money in the world plus marrying the person of your dreams. However, if your friends and family knew you would have this money in the future and started pressing you and making you feel guilty to give them money—even before you got your share—how would you feel? This is similar to how people may make you feel if they know you've given your heart to God. They act negatively towards you, but some may also be positively and sincerely happy for you and hope that you'll help them understand Christianity and salvation.

Whether we like it or not, we are all going to experience changes and discomfort at some point in our life. We should not be scared of God because of this. Likewise, periods of change usually bring some of the best times or most meaningful results we ever experience. When we get together with a new friend for the first time, it can be somewhat awkward, but it also can be more exhilarating than getting together with someone we have known for a long time. Most of us have been to parties or weddings where we hardly knew anyone. At first, everyone quietly stands around, sticking close to the few individuals they do know. Before the gathering is over, many people have met several new people and are having a great time.

I promise that God wants to be friends with each of us—regardless of what our life has been like. He is not out to humiliate or embarrass us. He has literally died trying to convince us of this. If you've never experienced real love, then God will find a way to show you what real love is. If you have experienced the incredible joy of love and being in love, please believe that your feelings of love are just a fraction of how much God loves you.

Summary

I want to acknowledge that there will be some who feel that I should be stopped from making a book like this available to people in an attempt to convert their religious views. For those who feel this way, I am willing to discuss their concerns and would be happy for them to try to convince me of their views. When the truth is presented, however, those who do not want to hear the truth will usually cover their ears and request to have the truth turned off. Someday, we will all have to face the truth, and for many that someday will be too late for them to change their final destiny. How will you spend eternity?

Chapter 14

A New Life

For those of you too young to remember life before digital cameras--there was a time where cameras required physical rolls of film. To actually see the pictures you snapped, you had to take this roll of film to a store—typically to the local pharmacy—fill out an envelope with your name and phone number, drop the film in the envelope, lick it to seal it, then drop it in a box inside the store. When the pictures were developed and ready for pickup a week or so later, the store would call and you only paid for the pictures at the time you picked them up.

When my older daughter was three years old, we needed to drop off film at a local pharmacy and she was excited to take on the task of jumping out of the car and dropping a prepared envelope inside the box at the store. She had seen her parents do it many times so she knew what to do. Unfortunately, when she got to the front of the store, her tiny three-year-old body wasn't big enough for the automated door sensor to detect her presence. She started to jump up and down in front of the door, but it wouldn't open. It was really cute watching her persistence. Finally, I got out of the car and stepped near the entrance and the door opened. I then waited for her to head back out so I could trigger the door again.

I'm happy to report that if you decide to reconcile yourself to God, no matter your size or age, God will gladly open the door for you. God's message of hope, often called the Gospel, is a powerful message that's life changing. However, it is simple enough for even a young child to understand.

The Bible indicates that if you have repented to God and turned your life over to Him—as if we ever really have control of our life anyway—you can trust that God will take care of you forever. Once Jesus came to live on this earth, this reconciliation to God gained special meaning. After Jesus' life, death, and resurrection, everyone who comes to God in the name of Jesus will have the Holy Spirit of God come be a part of their life and each person will be given a special talent or gift from God. There is no avoiding some change to our lives once we are reconciled to God. We can, however, choose to hide this change from everyone or we can choose to live out this change.

New Testament believers are called Christians and have the spirit of God within them, and thereby are capable of living lives of State 4 people who want to help everyone—even former enemies—become reconciled with them and with God. This special talent or gift that God gives us is for us to perform our role in helping this reconciliation process. My gift is in the area of evangelism and encouragement, but if you had known me in my pre-Christian life, you would probably never have expected me to be writing religious books or telling others about Jesus.

After we become Christians, we are not automatically going to change all aspects of our life the way God wants us to. In fact, we will probably struggle to hold onto certain pieces of our former life as long as we live on earth. Some, however, never really change outwardly in any area. They want to live in State 1 or 2, where their concerns are focusing on their own life instead of focusing on what God wants for their life.

In the last few decades, the world we live in has definitely gotten worse in some ways. Many people years ago did not lock their doors or take the keys out of their cars. We could not imagine doing this today. On the other hand, some things have gotten better. Nearly every city in America has local Christian radio stations that are very much on target with their doctrine and these stations truly have Christian love for people. While we have the ability to fill our minds with all sorts of junk from television, radio, and magazines, we also have the ability to fill our minds and hearts with more beneficial music and information than ever before. Before the technological revolution, a Christian would be lucky to hear two or three hours of teaching and Bible discussion in a week's time. Now it is possible to hear ten or more hours of Bible discussion each week via Christian radio and YouTube®, and these are by some of the most gifted pastors and teachers of our time rather than just from our one local pastor—even though he may be a fantastic pastor and teacher himself.

I will admit that I have some concerns about the television evangelists that most of us have been exposed to. While some of these have proven to be liars and con men, I have found most to be true men of God. Nevertheless, we should all be reading the Bible daily and thereby be able to determine for ourselves whether our local pastor or some other pastor is telling the truth. I cannot recommend a specific church to everyone who reads this book, but I do believe that every Christian needs to find a church home, since the church is the organization through which we minister to people and reach those who are unreconciled to God. I also recommend a person meet with the leadership of a prospective church to discuss the church's doctrine and purpose. Remember, all churches have their own personality. There hopefully will be several churches with sound doctrine and purpose where you live, so pick the one that best suits who you are and that can reach out to your friends and family who may be unreconciled to God.

Whether a person is in the process of finding a new church home, still contemplating Christianity, or a veteran Christian, the following sources should be very beneficial. I recommend a study version of one of the following English translations of the Bible.

- The New American Standard Bible (NASB)
- The New International Version (NIV)
- The New King James Version (NKJV)
- English Standard Version (ESV)

In addition to the Bible, here are some other sources that you may find very useful. First, Billy Graham produced numerous books and television and radio broadcasts. He certainly did more to change peoples' hearts for God than probably anyone else in our time, and he had a big impact on me in my early days of being a Christian. Another up-and-coming Christian leader is Francis Chan. He has a way of articulating life and death issues in very powerful and unique ways. You can easily find him on YouTube by searching for his name. Three of his most powerful messages that I've heard can be found at the following links

- https://youtube/2bs_ma68fE
- https://youtube/h3N0-pZ4pE4
- https://youtube/frR9LNmfRrc

There are some terrific Christian radio stations. I prefer those affiliated with Salem Communications. They have stations with excellent teaching ministries 24 hours a day and they also have a "Listen Live" feature on their website and a mobile app for smart phones. Since almost no one in the United States goes out to buy a radio for home or office use anymore, it's great to be able to listen to great radio anywhere on the planet that has Internet access or a cell-phone signal. My favorite Salem station is the San Francisco Bay Area's KFAX AM 1100, and you can download their mobile app.

Some wonderful radio pastors and teachers you can listen to include Dr. J. Vernon McGee, Dr. Chuck Swindoll, Dr. Charles Stanley, Dr. Ravi

Zacharias, and Dr. David Jeremiah. Most of them also have daily or weekly broadcasts on stations in almost every city throughout the country and even across the globe. Their doctrine is very sound, and the messages they present are usually the best information available about the Bible and the issues they discuss.

The books *Reason to Believe* by R. C. Sproul, *Answers to Tough Questions...* by Josh McDowell, and *The Answer Book* by Ken Hamm expand many of the questions and issues about Christianity that I have tried to explain.

Listed here are some very powerful books that you might also want to read:

- *What on earth am I here for* by Rick Warren
- *The Reason for God* by Tim Keller
- *Mere Christianity* by C. S. Lewis
- *Crazy Love* by Francis Chan
- *Chasing God: One Man's Miraculous Journey in the Heart of the City* by Roger Huang

These recommended resources are covered in more detail in the Suggested Resources and/or Bibliography sections at the back of the book.

My main reason for writing this book was to put together a resource that I could share with my family and friends, which hopefully explains the Bible, Christianity, and who God and Jesus are in ways that they can relate to. After years of discussing these matters verbally with people, I believe that my presentation accurately addresses most of the issues and concerns of those I come in contact with. Although many books have probably been written that better address some aspects of these matters, I so far have not been able to find one that completely appeals to me. I hope that within the next few years, many more books like this will be written, read, and distributed throughout the world.

It concerns me greatly how little effort there is by Christians to share information like this with people they know. It is interesting how many of us will get in a sales job or one of the popular network marketing businesses these days and quickly contact our family and friends to get them to buy whatever product we are selling. We gladly supply them with all sorts of books, tapes, and discussion about our product. Why is it then that most Christians will never make the effort to contact one person who is probably on course to spend eternity in hell and tell them about Jesus or hand them a book like this? Many churches do not even provide a Bible to new members or to new Christians—let alone supply information that its members can share with others. If we got a thousand dollars every time we handed out a book or discussed Jesus with someone, I wonder how many Christians and churches would suddenly get busy.

Communication with God

Let us not miss the most important matter of all. God loves us and our family and friends more than we can imagine. Through His Son Jesus, we are able to interact with the God and creator of our world. Although it is not His common mechanism to communicate to us by opening heaven and speaking directly to us, the Bible and the Holy

Spirit that dwells within Christians act like a "smart phone" from God to get information and responses from Him about the issues and concerns that go on in our daily lives. Likewise, prayer is sort of our way of transmitting information and responses to Him. If we are praying and expressing to God what our concerns, joys, and pains are—something that does not have to be a formal and tedious thing as many believe—God can and will respond to us, guide us, and help us. If we are reading the Bible, we are reading the responses He sends us about the prayers we are making. If we are attending a Christian church, we are able to serve God and do with our life what we were meant for.

Lastly, and most importantly, set aside time every day to read the Bible and to communicate with God as discussed previously in Chapter 13. Since the whole point to Christianity is enjoying the friendship God wants to have with us, the Bible and prayer are basically the only ways that are generally available to really spend time with God. If you give your heart to God, I promise that He will answer your prayers and the needs in your life. This communication will continue to strengthen your faith and trust in Him.

Likewise, prayer is fundamental to our basic faith. Although the Bible has passages that state that we should not put God to the test, I think this does not indicate that God does not want us to ask for His help, but rather that He does not want us to put ourselves in difficult and unnecessary situations to see if God really will get us through. If a believer chooses to be sexually promiscuous with the assumption that God will not allow pregnancy or disease to occur, then that person has misunderstood the relationship with God.

The Bible's Book of Luke, Chapter 3, has the story of Jesus being tempted by the devil. At one point, the devil suggests that Jesus jump off the high roof of the temple so that God could rescue Him from injury and show the crowds that Jesus was a person with special powers. Jesus responded that we are not to test God in this way. Instead, if someone asks God to help them through difficult situations or asks Him to help others who have a certain need, He will respond to the prayer if the request is consistent with His commandments. In the analogy of the believer having faith that God would prevent problems caused by promiscuous behavior, the correct prayer would be for the person to ask God to help them avoid the tempting situation. The obvious choice would be to flee from it quickly if faced with such temptation.

Prayer is also essential because—when it comes right down to it—it is the only real thing on which we can base our personal trust and faith in God. If we have had numerous prayers answered, our faith in God has solid basis. If we have had only one or two unusual events occur as answers to prayers we made, we may at times feel that these were possibly just coincidences. However, over my thirty-plus years as a Christian, I have had countless prayers answered.

One of the most amazing prayers that I ever had answered was the day I met my good friend, Harsh Jadhav. I had been living in California for about five years and had been asking God for several years to send me a really close friend. I had many close friends and family members when I lived in the south, and I had been used to calling them or visiting them quite often. Unfortunately, living in California with the time difference and distance made it very hard to catch up with my long-time friends by phone—let alone actually meet with them. They say that most people in America make their closest friends in high school and college. At forty years of age, I could say the same thing. I hadn't really added a close buddy in almost twenty years.

In June of 2005, I experienced the darkest day of my life when my wife of almost twenty years told me out of nowhere that she wanted a divorce. The very next day, I met Harsh at a work conference, and we immediately connected. He had gone through something similar a few years earlier, and he was able to help me cope with my situation. Over the past twelve-plus years, Harsh and I have rarely gone more than a few months without chatting by phone or meeting up in person. He has truly been like a brother to me, and God sent him into my life the day I needed that prayer answered most. Situations like this one—and countless others where things happened beyond just coincidence—have been very influential to my faith and to the faith of many others.

I personally believe that God puts us all to the test at certain times in our life. We all experience situations where we know what the right thing to do is, but we avoid doing it because we lack the faith that our right response will receive the short- and long-term rewards that we would like. For instance, it is easy for a nine-year-old to join in with other kids and pick on a classmate's handicap or weight problem—even though they may know it is not the right thing to do. They may fear that standing up for their classmate may cause them to also be ridiculed. If on the other hand, they have stood up for others in the past and have rarely been ridiculed for it, then they are much more likely to have faith that doing the right thing again in this situation will result in the best possible outcome.

A person who stands up for the innocent will probably develop or deepen a friendship with that individual and may develop or deepen friendships with others who knew it was not right to pick on this person. Until we ask God to help us through

ETERNITY

these types of situations and witness how God can and does cause things to work out in ways better than we could ever imagine, we will struggle with believing that there really is a loving personal God who cares about us.

As prayer is the foundation of our faith and belief in our personal and loving God, so too is Bible study. If your sweetheart or best friend took time to write you a letter or send you an e-mail each day that contained extremely useful information for you and required about fifteen minutes or so of your time, would you take the time to read your friend's personal messages and information? We need to think of Bible reading in this same way. Since God loves us so very much and has taken the time over the past thousands of years to have His word written down and translated into nearly every possible language, we have greatly misunderstood our relationship with God if we never find ourselves taking time to read the Bible.

Church Attendance

Although God does not show up visually and verbally at any church that I have ever attended, there is a special type of interaction and message from God that can only come from the family-like love and spirit of the church gathering, and it will be our loss if we miss it. Though health issues and other things sometimes prevent us from being at church, the idea of being a Christian but not wanting to be part of a church is contradictory. We do not all have the circumstances that allow us to attend a church with sound Christian doctrine, such as people in some countries, people in prison, and people with limited mobility, but we all can pray, we all can get a Bible, and we can all start our own church if none is available.

Finally, if you believe that you are a Christian because you have reconciled yourself to God, there is a test that should help you verify this. We spoke of the three questions that basically represent the entrance exam for heaven back in Chapter 7, but it can be summed up this way. If you have truly become a Christian, then there should be no one that you hope will spend eternity in hell. You should also show love and kindness to even those who are enemies or rivals to you. There should have been some change in your life comparable to a change in a relationship you might have with someone if they went from being an enemy of yours to being one of your closest friends, where Jesus represents that person who has now become your best friend. Also, it is critical to remember that once we reconcile ourselves to God, we are saved and will spend eternity in heaven—no matter what we do the rest of our life and regardless of what other influences and religions try to tell us. Once you give your heart to God, He will always watch over you in a special way, even when you know you're not being very lovable to Him or others.

So where will you spend eternity? Will you be in heaven? Will your family and friends and their family and friends be there also? I will be there only because I have asked God for forgiveness, invited Him into my heart, and been willing to obey Him. I haven't always been close to God since I invited Him into my heart more than 30 years ago, but nonetheless, He became my heavenly Father back then and has loved me like a son, even when I didn't deserve His loving kindness.

We never know how many breaths we have left. Remember how you felt the first time you had a crush on someone and wished so badly that you had the courage to say hello to them? What if you had the guts to say hello and that crush turned out to lead to a lifelong loving friendship and marriage? What if you let the opportunity go by and you always had to wonder what if you had said hello when you had the chance? If you've never given your heart to Jesus Christ, please say hello to Him now and I promise you'll be saying hello to the best friend you can ever imagine.

If you want to become a Christian right now, below is a prayer from Reverend Billy Graham that you may want to read to guide your thoughts and interactions with God the Father and His Son, Jesus Christ.

ETERNITY

> Dear God,
>
> I'm a sinner. I'm sorry for my sins. I want to turn from my sins. I believe Jesus Christ is your Son. I believe He died for my sin and that You raised Him to life. I want to trust Him as my Savior and follow Him as Lord from this day forward. Jesus, I put my trust in You and I surrender my life to You. Please come into my life and fill me with Your Holy Spirit. I pray this in the name of Jesus. Amen.

Congratulations! If you were sincerely praying to God using this prayer or something more personal but similar to this, you will have eternal life and will spend the afterlife in heaven. God has come into your heart and will be with you for the rest of your life and beyond. While you are not required to work to keep your salvation, it is critical that you let the Lord be your closest friend, that you read His word regularly, and that your life reflect true love for and obedience to Him. There may be days where you won't understand the difficult circumstances that life may bring you and there even may be times when you'll be angry with the Lord, but I promise that it will all make sense at some point in the future. Finally, don't ever let hatred and bitterness consume you. Regardless of what happens, it is so very critical that we love everyone, even those who have done horrible things to us or to others on this planet. Anyone can love their friends, but only a true child of God can love their enemies. Your love for your enemies will be the most important aspect in determining your eternal destination.

Summary

I hope this book has been a blessing to you. Please let me know your thoughts and feedback on this book. Also, please let me know if you have any questions that I could assist with, including help finding a great church near you. When you contact me, I will try to follow up with you within a few days. My email address is: russ@sc-love.org

Suggested Resources

(Please also refer to the Bibliography in the following section)

Books

The Ryrie Study Bible—New International Version (NIV). Ryrie, Charles Caldwell.

Mere Christianity. Lewis, C. S. This is a very powerful book about Christianity, and it addresses many issues that skeptics of Christianity wrestle with.

Reason for God. Tim Keller. This book addresses additional important questions about life and death, pain and suffering, and eternity. It is an excellent book that gives powerful clarity and insights about Christianity.

What on Earth Am I Here For. Rick Warren. This book was also called "The Purpose Driven Life" in earlier versions. It is one of the most popular Christian books of the past 3 decades. This book also gives terrific answers and insights into life's most important questions.

Chasing God: One Man's Miraculous Journey in the Heart of the City. Roger Huang. This book is the true story of a man who saw people desperately in need of food, clothing, and housing in the toughest inner-city section of San Francisco. Roger built an amazing revolutionizing ministry that provides food, schooling, and housing to thousands of people. His simple but compassionate ministry over the past 3 decades has led to many other ministries helping people around the globe.

SUGGESTED RESOURCES

The Answers Book—Answers to the 12 Most-Asked Questions on Genesis and Creation/Evolution. Ham, Ken; Snelling, Andrew; and Wieland, Carl.

The God Makers. Decker, Ed and Hunt, Dave. This book exposes the real beliefs and practices of the Mormon Church.

The Sacred Mushroom & the Cross. Allegro, John M. This book is a an interesting book for those who want to gain insights the minds of religious sceptics.

Armageddon, Oil and the Middle East Crisis. Walvoord, John F. This book examines the ongoing turmoil of the Middle East and describes the future events that the Bible predicts.

Turning Point: A Christian Worldview Declaration. Schlossberg, Herbert and Olasky, Marvin. This book discusses how everyone has a basic worldview that shapes their personal faith and philosophy and leads all of us to interpret information to fit our worldview—a person who believes in evolution

ETERNITY

has a religious faith of his own that causes him to interpret most scientific information to confirm his belief, while a person who believes in creationism can interpret the same data as support of his very different belief system.

Media

KFAX AM 1100 Radio Station (www.kfax.org): KFAX is a commercial AM radio station licensed to San Francisco, California, and heard on traditional radio broadcasts around the Bay Area. As of 2014, the station is owned by Salem Media Group and programs a Christian radio teaching and talk format. They can be listened to almost anywhere on the globe via the internet or via their cell phone app (search KFAX AM 1100).

YouTube (www.YouTube.com): YouTube is a free video sharing website that makes it easy to watch online videos and is considered the most popular video website in the world as of 2018. It is currently owned by Alphabet / Google.

SUGGESTED RESOURCES

Ministries

Billy Graham Ministry (www.BillyGraham.org): 877-247-2426. This well-known organization has touched possibly billions of lives throughout the world this century and has a wealth of great sources to help people know and share information about Christianity. His organization also has weekly radio broadcasts and numerous television broadcasts that are also carried in most U. S. cities.

Focus on the Family (www.FocusOnTheFamily.com): 800-232-6459. This organization was developed by Dr. James Dobson and has very informative daily radio broadcasts throughout nearly every major U.S. city and many foreign countries. Their radio broadcasts, books, and tape sources provide excellent information about many issues regarding Christianity and family matters, such as marriage advice, social issues, and other important topics.

InTouch Ministries (www.InTouch.org): 800-789-1473. This organization is led by Dr. Charles Stanley. He has been a pastor, author, and speaker for more than 5 decades. His messages are especially encouraging and he is famous for saying "obey God and leave the consequences to God".

Ravi Zacharias International Ministries (www.RZIM.org): 800-803-3829. This organization is led by international Christian speaker and author Dr. Ravi Zacharias. He also has weekly radio broadcasts in most U.S. cities and in many foreign countries. The strength of his messages is his ability to address difficult questions about Christianity and other religions and to provide human viewpoints.

Through the Bible Ministries (www.TTB.org): 1-800-652-4253. This organization was developed by the late Dr. J. Vernon McGee and is an ongoing replay of Dr. McGee's excellent five-year tape series that takes radio listeners through the entire Bible. This daily radio broadcast is also carried in most U.S. cities and in many foreign countries.

Turning Point (www.DavidJeremiah.org): 877-998-0222. This organization is led by Christian

Suggested Resources

pastor, speaker and author Dr. David Jeremiah. Dr. Jeremiah has developed extensive material about the Bible's book of Revelation and the "End Times".

The Urban Alternative (www.TonyEvans.org): 800-800-3222. This organization is led by pastor Dr. Tony Evans. Daily radio broadcast are carried in most U.S. cities. Dr. Evans has a tremendous ability to explain difficult Biblical matters in very practical, understandable ways.

Tapes

The Subject Everybody Ignores. Swindoll, Charles. This audio message discusses the reality of hell and was the source for much of my discussion about hell in Chapter 11, "The Afterlife?"

Videos

Francis Chan. Francis Chan is a pastor and speaker who has recorded some of the most powerful and insightful messages about Christianity. I highly recommend his messages and they can currently be

ETERNITY

found on YouTube ® - here are the links to some of his greatest recordings:

- https://youtube/2bs_ma68fE
- https://youtube/h3N0-pZ4pE4
- https://youtube/frR9LNmfRrc

Jesus of Nazareth. This movie directed by Franco Zeffirelli with a major Hollywood cast is one of the best portrayals of Jesus Christ that I have seen. Some important aspects to Jesus' life and ministry are left out or not explained very well, but for the most part, this movie does an excellent job of identifying who Jesus is and what His life on this earth was probably like. It also shows what the nation of Israel physically and spiritually was probably like. This movie should be available in media from online sites such as Amazon.

Bibliography

Allegro, John M. *The Sacred Mushroom & the Cross.* Doubleday & Company, Inc., 1970.

Bandow, Doug. *Beyond Good Intentions—A Biblical View of Politics.* Wheaton, IL: Crossway Books, 1988.

Behe, Michael. *Darwin's Black Box.* New York: Simon & Schuster, 1996.

Billingsley, K. L. *The Seductive Image—A Christian Critique of the World of Film,* Wheaton, IL: Crossway Books, 1989.

Cahill, Mark (2011-11-29). One Second After You ... Die. Mark Cahill. Kindle Edition.

Decker, Ed and Hunt, Dave. *The God Makers.* Eugene, OR: Harvest House Publishers, 1984.

Goldner, Kathryn A. and Vogel, Carole G. *Why Mount St. Helens Blew Its Top,* Dillon Press, 1981, pp. 14–15.

Ham, Ken; Snelling, Andrew; and Wieland, Carl. *The Answers Book—Answers to the 12 Most-Asked Questions on Genesis and creation/Evolution.* Green Forest, AR: Master Books, 1990.

Laszlo, Ervin. *Evolution, The Grand Synthesis.* Boston, MA, Shambhala Publications, Inc., 1987, pp. 71.

Lehman, J. P. *The Proofs of Evolution.* London: Gordon & Cremonesi Publishers,1977.

Lewis, C. S. *Mere Christianity.* New York: MacMillan Publishing Company, 1952.

Libby, Willard F. *Radiocarbon Dating.* Chicago: The University of Chicago Press,1955, pp. 8–9.

Lindsey, Hal. *The Promise.* Eugene, OR: Harvest House Publishers, Inc., 1982.

McDowell, Josh and Stewart, Don. *Answers to Tough Questions Skeptics ask about the Christian Faith.* Wheaton, IL: Tyndale House Publishers, 1980.

O'Dea, Thomas F. *The Mormons.* Chicago: Chicago Press, 1957.

Pearcey, Nancy R. and Thaxton, Charles B. *The Soul of Science.* Wheaton, IL: Crossway Books, 1994.

Ryrie, Charles Caldwell. *The Ryrie Study Bible— New International Version.* Chicago: Moody Press, 1986.

Schlossberg, Herbert and Olasky, Marvin. *Turning Point: A Christian Worldview Declaration.* Wheaton, IL: Crossway Books, 1987.

Sproul, R. C. *Reason to Believe.* Grand Rapids, MI: Zondervan, 1978.

Swindoll, Charles. *The Subject Everybody Ignores.* (Audio Cassette) Insight for Living, Frisco, Texas, 1995.

Walvoord, John F. *Armageddon, Oil and the Middle East Crisis.* Grand Rapids, MI: Zondervan Publishing House, 1990.

____, *The New English Bible with the Apocrypha.* New York: Oxford University Press, 1971.

____. *You Can Live Forever in Paradise on Earth.* New York: Watchtower Bible and Tract Society of New York, Inc., 1989.

About the Author

Russ Walsh is a committed Christian with a heart to reach the lost with the Good News of Jesus Christ. Russ was born in South Carolina and grew up in a Gospel-preaching Baptist church. He committed his life to Christ at the age of twenty. He now lives in the San Francisco Bay Area. Russ currently leads cyber security compliance for one of the world's largest companies.

He has developed many innovative products and solutions in his career and has worked for companies such as IBM, EY, and several successful startups. He has also provided consulting services for every major technology company of our era, including Facebook, Apple, Google, Microsoft, Uber, Salesforce, Oracle, and Hitachi. He is the father of two daughters and has led many of his closest friends and family members closer to the Lord. He is an outspoken advocate of Jesus Christ and he is the founder of Sharing Christ's Love Ministry. Russ hopes to leverage new technology and Christian leaders to reach everyone on the globe with Christ's love.

God Bless.